CREATE AND PROTECT YOUR WEALTH
**WITH ACCESSIBLE STRATEGIES FOR
EVERYONE — EVERYWHERE**

THE
SWISS
WEALTH
CREATION

A Comprehensive Guide
for a New Era of Investment

RETO WINKLER

&

GISBERT REUTER

A variety of companion resources, including Guided Investor Type Worksheets, and other bonus materials, are included with your purchase of this book:

Go to

www.swisswealthcreation.com/free-bonus

and access all your free material.

CONTENTS

Part II: Mastering your Art of Investment

Module 1 — Cash Reserves

Part III: The Three Most Important Lessons 219

Part IV: What Can Be Your Next Step? 257

DISCLAIMER | EXCLUSION OF LIABILITY

The contents and information in this book reflect the personal opinions and views of the authors at the time of publication, which may differ from other publications. The reports are based exclusively on the personal experiences of the authors.

No warranties, representations or guarantees of any kind are made with respect to the content and information contained or referenced in this book, in particular with respect to its accuracy, completeness and timeliness. The content of external works or websites referred to directly or indirectly in this book is outside the responsibility of the authors.

Any liability claims for any losses, costs or damages (including consequential damages) resulting directly or indirectly from or in connection with the knowledge or use of the content and information provided or referenced in this book or caused by incomplete or incorrect information are excluded.

Trading in assets, financial products and other investment instruments and investing in such involves risks and can lead to high financial losses and total losses. The reader bears full and sole responsibility for his/her financial decisions. Past performance is not a reliable indicator of future performance. There is no certainty that the desired investment objectives will be achieved for any of the investment opportunities or portfolio designs discussed in the book. The reader is free to seek professional advice before making investment decisions. This book is not a substitute for such professional advice.

It is not a purchase offer or investment advice: The contents and information in this book are for informational purposes only and are intended to enhance the reader's understanding of how to deal with inflation. It does not constitute financial or investment advice and should not be construed as an investment recommendation or an invitation, solicitation, offer or recommendation to buy or sell securities, financial products or other investment instruments or to engage in any other transactions.

INTRO
THE SETUP

IT IS ALL ABOUT
TRUST

Let's get right to the point:

While there are various strategies for hedging against inflation, a common approach is to invest in assets that tend to perform well during periods of inflation, such as real estate, commodities like gold or oil, and inflation-protected securities like Treasury Inflation-Protected Securities (TIPS). These assets have historically shown the potential to retain or increase their value as inflation rises.

This book will show you several ways to use these strategies even if you have NEVER invested a dime, and even if you have lost a lot of money on bad decisions in your past.

Even if you have made a million mistakes, this book will help you through tough times and you will find it easy to achieve results! But there is more to it than a few common procedures or best practices. As you probably know, the Swiss did not invent banking, nor did they rethink it.

But they did add something very important.

The Swiss have enriched the banking industry with a unique trait that has always been known across borders.

I am talking about quality, which is why 35% of the world's private and institutional assets are managed in Switzerland. I am talking about trust. And that's what this book is about.

We want to bring trust back into your life, even or especially because there is so much mistrust, uncertainty, and corruption out there that we need to buckle up and grab the bull—aka inflation—by the horns. Let's do it now! Here's to the best results for your assets:

WHAT IF EVERYTHING WAS DIFFERENT TOMORROW?

What if the television suddenly told you the truth? What if those who are still trying to exert power and control over you today were a thing of the past tomorrow? What if YOU could do what you want, how you want, where you want, and with whom you really want, without asking anyone's permission?

What would your life be like if you could benefit from a plausible way to hedge against inflation and create wealth with a system that works for you?

I know this may sound like utopia or hopium but let me assure you that we do believe it is quite the opposite.

Look, this is what life is like today:

"I have bad news. The member states and the European partners have come to an agreement. It means that probably, not long from now the digital identity in the European Union will be affected. Right after this agreement, we have a digital identity wallet and we must put something in it and what this means is the digital euro, also known as the central bank, digital currency. And this is a very bad development."—This is what Rob Roos, Member of the European Parliament, posted on his X (formerly Twitter) account.

Now hear our answer: 3 times, yes!

Yes: That's a problem!

Yes: Big data, finance, and those in control will hate this book because it gives you power, awareness and confidence. Because...

Yes: There is a solution. And this book shows you how!

WHO IS THIS BOOK FOR?

This is an introduction from the desk of Gisbert Reuter. If you are like me, you see that governments and financial institutions are eroding our freedom and that there are a number of troubling changes, such as the increasing influence and power of large financial institutions in the global economy. If you are concerned that these institutions have become too large and have the potential to have a significant impact on financial markets and economies, you should carefully read the ideas we share in this book.

If you are concerned about growing income inequality and wealth concentration, and you see that governments and financial institutions play a key role in exacerbating these problems through policies and practices that benefit the powerful, you may want to learn how to create a level of wealth that gives you a little more freedom to respond to the external drama in your own way. Whether that means having the freedom to relocate your livelihood, or simply being able to pay the best doctors for your health instead of following the sick ideas of some health ministers or the WHO, is up to you.

Not only do you want to hedge against inflation, but you also want to build a moat to protect your rights! From the elimination of the gold standard in exchange for the ability of banks to lend money without reserves, to the use of lockdowns, QR codes, injections, and other invasions of your privacy as a means of control, you want to be in the best possible position to prevent all of these emerging threats from harming you, or at least doing the least amount of damage to your wealth and well-being. The same goes for your family and your closest friends. Inspire your world for better solutions. A Better Earth is possible for everyone!

When you agree that the confiscation of wealth through the automatic exchange of information and the presumption of guilt until proven innocent are egregious trends that we need to counteract, then not only should you read this book, but you should share it with the people you love. They don't have to be like-minded people. It is also quite possible that one or the other will see the light when the content we share in this book is shared with people who were previously skeptical of any criticism of the mainstream.

WHO IS THIS BOOK NOT FOR?

If you are the kind of person who likes to believe what the media, your Secretary of Health and Human Services, your Secretary of the Treasury, and those who actually own "your" money (that is, your bank, if you have it in there) say, then you now have three choices:

First, believe in the system you are a part of and put the book aside. It has somehow found its way to you, but the information in it can only confuse you more, and then it won't help you. Your mind is closed. Fiat brainwashed. The system wins!

Second, feel the need to open your mind and play with the content of the chapters before you. Don't take our word for it. Give it a test run. Examine your feelings as you read about things you've never seen or thought about before. Don't believe my words—somehow it does not feel very good to say, "Don't believe Reto's words, either", but yes, this is exactly what I want to suggest—please believe your feelings! They can change the course of your life.

Third, wait until the situation in your life reaches a level where you are forced to adapt to some change. That change always begins with new thinking. When it comes to excellent Wealth Creation and the best Inflation Hedge, remember this book and you will instinctively know that this is where you will find new thoughts that you may need to examine. When it is your time, read it, and as I said before: Don't believe Reto, don't believe my words, believe your feelings. They can change the course of your life.

WHY SHOULD YOU READ THIS BOOK?

It gives you faith in yourself and it teaches you things they don't want you to know. *The Swiss Wealth Creation* transforms your financial fears into know-how, do-how, and confidence! And it creates the trust that you need to stand firm.

We support you in not giving in. This book will create the strength that you need to not subordinate yourself. Your grit is the foundation of your own power, your prosperity, your growth, your future, your freedom!

And best of all, you can read it repeatedly, and you don't have to ask anyone's permission.

People give up freedom of choice in exchange for free shipping and a money-back guarantee.

They give their data to those in control, who turn it into chains that fit better and are more convenient.

WE WRITE THIS BOOK IN THE CONFIDENCE THAT WE CAN HELP YOU BREAK THESE CHAINS!

You will learn in this book how to become your own bank and how *The Swiss Wealth Creation* can mean 10X, 100X, 500X, or even 1000X for your own economy—depending on how many people want to be free with you. We are writing this book for you to bring trust and freedom back into your life.

We are writing this book - *together with you* - to bring trust and freedom to the world! Because when they can't control your money, they can't control you. Because when they can't control our money, they can't control us. Without losing control, we might be able to get our future back on track.

Let's weaken their control, strengthen our freedom, and help everyone.

That is Swiss Inflation Hedge. That is *The Swiss Wealth Creation.* Trust!—For Freedom—For Life!

So, here's to your wealth:

Reto Winkler & Gisbert Reuter

LET TRUST
TAKE THE LEAD
NAVIGATING
INFLATION
WITH THE SWISS
WEALTH CREATION

Protecting your wealth in times of inflation is a must if you want to get through tough times as well as possible. The problem is most people fail because they don't know how to properly hedge their assets even in times of economic stability. Key fact number one is that all your efforts will be for naught if you act now without a well-structured and plausible plan. Part of your problem is that you were told lies about financial planning from an early age, which makes it even more difficult to plan properly when times get tough.

At this very moment, the world is going through the biggest change it has ever seen, and not only in the financial sector; the effects will be felt in no other sector more severely than in your own pocket. More precisely, in your own economy! Add to this the challenge of key fact number two — that most of the world's current leaders don't meet the demands and needs of the digital age. Linear thinking is colliding with exponential times, and far too many business leaders are not thinking about the social component. Too few companies are creating impact for life.

Global meltdowns start at the periphery, like the Austrian Creditanstalt in 1931 or the collapse of Lehman Bros. in September 2008. The Federal Reserve's decision on June 15 to implement the largest interest rate hike in nearly 30 years, while financial markets are already collapsing, now guarantees a global depression and worse.

....

What this means for you is: Don't wait until it's too late. Respond immediately. Respond NOW!

....

Uncertainty and hyperinflation (and no small amount of corruption) get in the way of striving in times like these. Now, more than ever, you can lose your money, or someone can take it from you, until you have no honest, sound medium of exchange, no unit of account, and no safe store of value. You see currency debasement and inflation everywhere. Prices are rising very, very fast and billions of people can't afford the things they need. Do you really want to see the day when you must choose between paying your rent or buying food? Many people will probably have to make this decision much sooner than they can imagine, and it is not an issue to be taken lightly.

What this really means for you is: Your wealth is at risk!

Unconscionability, fraud, and institutional depravity are occurring in many ways, with serious implications for your economy and the lives of those you love and those who follow you.

So how would it feel to regain certainty in uncertain times?

HERE IS THE GOOD NEWS:

While everyone else out there is struggling, you only need to be a few steps ahead to create an unparalleled advantage for your financial future. "In the land of the blind, the one-eyed man is king," they say, and, yes, there are ways to store your value in safe forms, in a unique set as a medium of decentralized exchange, and as a unit of account.

There are ways to hedge your assets like (not only) the Swiss do. Imagine being able to benefit from the knowledge and experience of this wonderful little country, which is one of the last stands on earth for freedom and independence. You know, Switzerland didn't invent or reinvent banking, but Swiss banks have created a global pole position in TRUST, and that's exactly what you get when you use *The Swiss Wealth Creation System*.

Not only will you become a sought-after advisor at every party and social event, you will also be able to create wealth and navigate inflation in the best possible way.

The Swiss Wealth Creation shows you various ways to become a skilled investment luminary and create your own economy. **This book will give you an advantage over millions of others out there.**

PART I
OPEN YOUR MIND

WHEN YOU HAVE A LOYAL BANK
YOU *ARE* A LOYAL BANK!

Hey, this is Gisbert Reuter again. Let me jump right in and tell you why you are most likely a safe bank!

You see, when customers trust and remain loyal to a bank, it indicates that the bank is doing something right in terms of providing quality services, meeting customer needs, and building strong relationships. Loyalty is an important factor in the banking business. But is it the bank's loyalty that really counts, or is it your loyalty as a customer that the bank really wants? You will notice that Reto and I are writing this book a little differently than you may be used to. This is good. It opens you up to the new! We are writing this book over a great cup of coffee, and we are going to go through *The Swiss Wealth Creation* like a conversation between friends.

So, when you as a customer are loyal to a bank, you are more likely to continue using its services, recommend it to others, and maintain a long-term relationship. This loyalty can result in various benefits for the bank, such as increased customer retention, higher customer lifetime value, and positive word-of-mouth referrals.

You, as a loyal customer, indicate that the bank has successfully built a relationship with you, provided satisfactory experiences, and met your customer expectations. This loyalty can be a result of factors such as personalized customer service, competitive products and rates, convenient banking channels, and effective problem resolution.

Furthermore, you, as a loyal customer, and as a piece of their customer base, can contribute to the bank's overall reputation and brand image. Positive customer experiences and loyalty can enhance the bank's credibility and attract new customers who value trust and reliability.

In summary, *when you have a loyal bank—you are a loyal bank* is a part of the banker's business strategy, and many people out there do not see these aspects.

Side note: Could I teach you anything about being a bank customer if I, like millions of others, had been stuck with just one or two banks in my life, since my first job, or since I was a kid? Probably not. But in my life, the opposite is true. I am kind of the opposite of "a loyal bank" or a loyal bank customer, so I could teach you a lot (!!!) and unveil a whole lot of BS (bankshit). I will tell you why: I went from Germany, where I was born, to the Canary Islands at a very early age. Later, I lived in South America and had a business in Toronto. So, in more than 30 years in business, I have worked with many banks, in four countries, and on three continents. The journey (or should I say odyssey) began in the German Sparkasse, when, as a first grader, they won me over with their piggy bank and made me believe: "You can't handle the contents as well as we can, so give it to us and we'll even give you 5 marks in your free savings account." Isn't this belief strongly integrated in hundreds of millions or even billions of subconscious minds?

Know that at the age of 5 or 6, your subconscious simply accepted everything you were told, and from that day on, it's one of your programs: Prompt: YOU CAN'T HANDLE MONEY. GIVE IT TO THE BANK. THEY ARE THE ONLY ONES WHO KNOW HOW! This is by far the most important point of financial education for everyone. Also consider the fact that more education about money is, let's say, "generally rare" in the educational system. So I say "thank you, Sparkasse" for this lousy, hard-to-crush, un-wealth program.

I have been a customer of Deutsche Bank, Santander, Banca March, Solbank, Banco de Sabadell, BBVA, Bancolombia, and TD Bank in Canada, and I will miss one or two of them.

Now: I have a golden rule: If I can't say anything good about someone, I don't say anything!

But, as always and everywhere, there are exceptions, even at banks. My current long-term business relationship manager at the German Volksbank is one of those exceptional examples. The world should have more like you, Mr. Siegel. Thank you for all the great work and support! And comdirect (online-only branch of

Commerzbank AG) has also been at my side for many years and is a perfect example of how banks should work. So, I would like to take this opportunity to thank both of them: it is very important these days to focus on the great things so that your attention is not diverted to all the negatives out there. These two great banking experiences irrevocably eclipse all others.

I would also like to thank my author-colleague and friend, Jens Krautscheid, for recommending comdirect. I think it was back in 2006 or 2007 in a Rule Number One seminar when you taught me about stocks and trading — a skill that has saved "my life" and that of my family twice to date! I am full of gratitude for all the things I learned from you. My experience with comdirect was actually the first time in my life that I was 100% surprised and happy with banks. And yes, I have been loyal to them for more than 16 years.

Which brings me back to you, Reto: Thank you for letting me take this trip into my past. I want you to explain why it is the bank's strategy to have loyal customers. Why does it reflect positively on the bank itself? Why is it a fact that loyalty indicates that the bank is meeting customer needs, building strong relationships, and providing satisfactory experiences? And: Can this loyalty translate into benefits for the bank beyond increased customer loyalty and positive brand reputation?

This is a wonderful question to start with, Gisi. Yes, of course! This is an important issue. The bank definitely knows the benefits of loyalty. After all, it's all about trust, and you can be 100% confident that the bank's loyalty is a business plan that really works. A bank knows that it pays to create a massive, binding relationship. So, the main binding element is trust, not manipulation.

When you were a little boy, you traded your piggy bank for a bank account. The bank even gave you 5 dollars, or francs, or euros! You'll never forget this generous gesture from a complete stranger. He's been your banker ever since. You trust him. Over and over again, you put money into your bank account from somewhere, you go to the bank with your parents, and the banker tells them what you need to invest, and so you build a relationship with your banker. And because you only work with one bank, they can always see exactly what you have in your account.

Then he advises you very early as a teenager, and he tells you: "Why don't you take a youth savings account? You'll get one percent more interest than on the normal salary account." And then you have this and that advantage, and then you start saving, which, in fact, is a good thing.

But the money you've saved then sits in your bank account, and when you have more money in your account later - when you're in education and more money comes into your account after your studies - you often get a call from your banker saying, "You know, you have a certain amount of money here. We should really sit down and see what we can tweak here!"

At this point, you usually have no idea what your options are. But, of course, you know this from your parents: the banker takes good care of your money—that is his job—so "you choose" some bank products that offer promising interest rates, and then you take out your first life insurance policy and start saving. They show you how all your assets will build up over the decades, from 20 to 65, and so you pay into your savings plan, usually with a standing order, and then the subject quickly falls by the wayside or is completely forgotten because you take care of all the issues that accompany you in life, especially in your younger years. Your friends, going out, your job, your education.

As a result, you often have only one exposure to investing, and that is on the sidelines. You make your first investments through the bank and its products. Then you start a family and want to buy your own home; a small, single-family home. You go back to your banker. He makes you a very good offer because he knows your numbers inside out, because he has been watching them closely for the last ten or fifteen years. So, he knows exactly what you need, how you work, what your situation is, and of course, you get a very special offer that he has coordinated with his boss. The interest rate is even a little bit lower than the official one in the bank brochure, and you're very happy.

In this way, the bank binds you more and more to it. Because for all the security that your bank naturally demands, you now must raise the monthly amounts of your life insurance policy so that the whole thing is properly secured, and your loyalty to the bank is built up. You pay your mortgage until you're 50 or 55. When you have some money left over, the bank calls you again and says, "Hello, sir or madam, we've seen that you have $10,000 or $20,000 in your account. We have a great savings product here; it's a great fund that you should invest in. Look, why don't we reallocate it? Just come over and we'll talk things through..." And yes, because it's not too much money and because your dear banker actually takes the time to talk to you personally and even has a coffee and a cookie for you, you do what he wants!

Then you sign the paperwork and let the whole thing go as your bank advises. And then come the first interviews at the age of 60, when you get another request from your banker. Then they say: "Look, we need to do some retirement planning. Here's what it looks like, we have these options with these and these products..." You know you're in good hands.

There's a risk profile that you must fill out, and interestingly enough, there are always a lot of red text parts. There are a lot of exclamation points, and a lot of risks to scare you subconsciously, so you're glad you have your banker on your side to give you good advice. With all this manipulation, you just have to trust your bank—who else? The best thing to do is not to take any initiative at all, but just take the bank's safe product. And those who tell you otherwise are all scoundrels and criminals who just want your money. Of course, the bank doesn't! And that's how they get involved in retirement planning with you. When the time comes for you to retire, you do it through your banker because so far, everything has worked out well, and then you get your pension, and so on until the end of your life.

That's how the banks build a very strong relationship with you. They don't allow anything to come in from the outside.

If you ever come up with an idea of your own, they immediately raise the big risk sheet that you have to take into account, and you are constantly discouraged from looking at other things. This is the normal scenario that plays out in the life of a bank customer who, from an early age, is simply tied to the bank and driven by the press, by the media, by employers, by politicians, and, above all, directly by the banks to stay with their bank and to invest in the industry's products instead of learning how to invest their money successfully themselves.

You can learn this, and I promise you that once you do apply what you get from us here in this book, you will also learn how to consistently beat your bank's returns!

We will catch up with that topic later. You will learn how to become your own bank!

A CHALLENGE AWAITS
UNRAVELING YOUR PROBLEM NUMBER ONE

The main problem I see is that people have money in bank accounts, and they lose money by keeping it in the bank account. We at Winkler Global Wealth show our private advisory clients how to put their money to work like the big players do.

What we do is, you and I sit down, and we come up with a customized strategy for you to not only preserve the value of your hard-earned money, but to actually make more money with what I call *The Swiss Wealth Creation*. So, it's not just about protecting your wealth and hedging against inflation, it's also about growing your wealth.

The #1 problem is not that you have money in the bank. Your top problem is having money in the bank while the world's economy is dealing with inflation:

Look: When you have money in the bank, it means you have saved it for later. But when the world economy is facing inflation, you have a problem with your savings.

Your money is being eaten up! Inflation means that the prices of things - your rent, your food, your clothes, your cost of living - keep going up over time. But the money you have in the bank today will be worth less tomorrow. Look at your life and see what happens with your purchases—do prices go up or down?

What about your grocery bills? What about gasoline? Heating costs? What about your rent? Are the costs going down or up? Everywhere you look, you notice that where you might have paid 100 Swiss Francs (or Dollars or Euros) for something a year ago, you are paying 150, 200 or more today—for the same thing!

While this is your reality outside your bank, the money inside it is a trap! There are two points to this. Inflation eats up your money; it will take a couple of decades and the amount you have in your savings account will be worth nothing. And—as if that were not enough—the other side is that banks charge you for their expenses, and their expenses are huge.

Reto, I am jumping in here because there is one more thing the reader absolutely needs to know: When it comes to "your" money at banks, owning the money you have in your bank account is a little different from owning other physical objects. When you deposit money in a bank account, it becomes a liability of the bank. You are simply no longer the owner of the money; you are a creditor of the bank. This is a wonderful thing in both of our mother tongues (and it is exactly the same in Swiss German and in German): creditor is "Gläubiger" and the

German word *Gläubiger* literally means "the one who believes" in something. You will learn in this book why believing in your bank is not a good business plan, just as believing in God is not enough to run a successful business. You must do something more, don't you agree?

Yes, I believe in God, too! But when it comes to money and wealth creation, I prefer to trust plausible mechanisms.

A very good mechanism for creating plausible wealth is the creation of value chains that benefit everyone. The more people involved who directly benefit from these ventures, the more plausible and certain success becomes.

"In God We Trust," as the Greenback says, is wonderful, but it doesn't create wealth! Trust is good as long as no one takes away your property, right? But what if inflation is driven by a few to consistently and congruently take power away from those who undoubtedly (or unwisely) believe (in banks or God)? And what if inflation is a tool that serves a few, but certainly not you?

Well, to make a long story short, when that is the case, there is one guaranteed result: Sooner or later, your money will be gone! Okay, it won't be gone; it's just that someone else will have it.

So be clear about this truth. When you give your money to the bank, it is no longer your property. The money in your bank account is the bank's money. You are the creditor. You are giving credit to the bank. Haven't you believed all your life that it should be the other way around? Even though this means that the bank is—at least in theory—responsible for keeping your money safe and making it available to you when you need it, there are better ways.

And be aware that you have, depending on your bank, limits for withdrawals. My savings account with 0.75% interest allows withdrawals up to CHF 50,000 per year without a period of notice! If I want more of my money back, I need to give them a notice 3-months in advance. A bonus savings account with 1% interest (per year!) is even worse: CHF 20,000 per year, everything above with a 6-month notice period... Are you serious? This is my money! And I have to beg for it? At least with a regular checking account with 0.1% interest there is a CHF 50,000 withdrawal limit per month, above a 3-month notice period. This gives some flexibility.

Reto, please tell us about your experiences! You were not always a successful investor. And I think that is one of the biggest takeaways for the reader. It's not that you were born with a golden spoon in your mouth. You went through huge learning curves, and that's exactly what I look for when it comes to who can be the best mentor for me in a particular area. How can someone mentor me if they don't know what it's like to have the problem I have with a particular issue? Reto, you've lost some serious money, haven't you? It took some trial and error before you really learned the do-how and know-how of successful wealth creation. Please let us be a part of that learning curve.

Sure, Gisi. It is my absolute pleasure and honor to share my story. I believe that even my biggest setbacks are for the benefit of others, because sharing my failures can prevent others from going down the same path. May it be of the greatest benefit to you, dear reader, that I share even my darkest moments with you.

MY FIRST TIME:
A GREAT START WITH A TRAGIC END

When I first learned how to make money without always trading my time for money, it was in network marketing. I grew into a leadership position where my wife and I had a large team of business partners. We took the first big step in our network business. I say it was a big step because we were able to show other people what they could do. Because we took our leaders to a level that was a wonderful achievement for them. They were all able to create and benefit from their passive income.

The next big step on my learning curve came when I started in US real estate. I went into a niche market called tax deeds. In the US, people get tax liens if they do not pay their property taxes, and they get the lien on their house. And after a certain period of time, depending on the state, these houses are sold in an auction called a tax deed auction, and of course, you can buy these houses in these tax deed auctions.

So that's where I came in: I bought 25 houses at different auctions for a group of allies, and we worked with them. That was a club deal. A club deal is when you bring a group of investors to the table for a specific investment purpose. There were three of us who did the work. The others were just passive investors, and we bought these houses and fixed them up. We flipped them. And we created solid returns for all the investors. They all doubled their investment that they had in our group. With the first property, we made a 34% gain in 134 days: WOW! I made all these friends and contacts an annual return of 93%! It just felt like I was king of the world. Of course, this was not supposed to last too long. But it just felt great. Especially since you are taught all your life that investments up to 6% return are safe and anything above that is just high risk. It felt crazy to see why the rich are getting richer; to see with my own flesh and blood that it's just a matter of thinking outside the box and looking for the opportunities, and then taking action and doing it.

It was an unbelievably great feeling to have that experience that it really works. That it's not just something that they tell you from a stage or in some book. The experience that it really works, that you can get these kinds of returns—man, like 93% in just one year! It was mind-blowing. I just keep doing it and the world is ours. And even if not, even if the return is just 10x, I would just continue to crush it.

Just put yourself in my shoes: You are the head of this club deal, so you have all the inside and outside information. And now you have the privilege of informing all the people that they just made a 93% return on their investment. There is nothing that feels better, I can tell you that.

The inner circle, two of my closest friends, got the information first. It was between 9 p.m. and midnight. I set up the meeting and I think we made it around 10 p.m. because Thomas, one of the two buddies, had a small child and at that time, the child was asleep. So, when we got on a Zoom call and saw each other, we saw the smiles on our faces and the laughter, and I also showed them over and over again the screen with the bank account income statement that was really there. We just cheered a little bit late at night. It was so exciting that we just couldn't sleep.

It was so much fun to talk to them and tell them that it worked, and from there, we went out and told all the other investors, and it was such a happy moment for all of us to see what was possible in this market. It took me about 12 years to get to that point, and I was incredibly thrilled with the outcome. I will never forget how it felt to deliver that news. You just believe that now, nothing can stop you. You just become invincible.

But you never are. And you are least of all when you feel so unbeatable, because then you start making mistakes. In the long run, it turned out to be a nightmare. We put so much money into these houses, and it took way too long for the lawyer to do the legal stuff. Then I ended up not being able to sell them. I had to sell them at a loss.

It was a great, great start and it was a tragic end, with me losing a lot of money.

But it made me learn some priceless lessons:

YOU ARE ALWAYS GREEDY

Don't try to get rid of greed. Learn how to handle it!

The bigger the returns were, the greedier I got, and even though I knew I was greedy, I just wanted more. So, learning to deal with greed is one of the most important topics for you if you want to become a very successful investor. I believe this single chapter alone can make you—or break you! Mastering greed has much more to do with your relationship with yourself than it does with managing your finances. However, it's essential to learn how to handle greediness in a healthy way. Just to be fully transparent, I think this is a lifetime process; the learning curves can be steep, or sometimes they are flat, but we never stop learning generosity, compassion, and humility, and becoming more pure humans.

I know that you, Gisi, are one of the best luminaries in the world for teaching people how to create and maintain excellent relationships. In all our time together and the wonderful work we have been doing for years, as well as all the great benefits you bring to other people's lives, I have always noticed and admired how much you focus on the relationship your private mentoring clients have with themselves. Would you say that in order to learn how to best manage greed, the relationship the reader has with himself or herself is the most important place to start?

Perhaps you would like to share your wealth of wisdom and experience on how to reprogram the subconscious mind and create a much more flourishing relationship with others based on what we can all change within ourselves.

Of course—isn't it true that the relationship we have with ourselves is the one we all care for the least and neglect the most? Just listen very carefully some days to yourself. How is your self talk? Is it full of admiration and love? Do you honor yourself and congratulate yourself for the things that you are good at, or are you most likely your biggest critic, telling yourself day in and day out how bad you are at whatever you do? Just observe yourself, don't judge. I only ask you to be honest with yourself.

If you are like most people I know and have worked with, you are probably your own worst critic. I bet there are few people in your life that you are as hard on as you are on yourself. And even when life is good and what you're doing is creating huge successes, I imagine you are not too different from most other entrepreneurs who are constantly acting as their own biggest discouragers.

I don't even want to go into emotional territory and thought processes at a time when we all have our fear buttons pushed. The world can be a terrible place to be in these times, and keeping your spirits up is a challenge. But you don't even need inflation or a hostile environment to be your worst enemy.

Whether you're an employee or entrepreneur, you notice various challenges or obstacles emerging amidst the opportunities that require your attention and careful management.

You are aware of all the intricate details and processes involved. You acknowledge that things may not always align perfectly with your expectations. In business, you tend to be self-critical.

Now, when it comes to investing, it gets worse! Because now you will perhaps not only fail in what you do, you could lose the fruits of what you did before, and it—of course—is your hard-earned money. You have earned it even though you were your biggest critic in the process. So it is, on the other hand, very easy to switch to the other extreme of the same vertical axis and pivot from criticism to greed. We all tend to move too far to one or another side of the same axis instead of aligning ourselves with the middle where things are simply balanced.

The good news is that you can learn to do it much better, and it is not difficult. You will learn everything you need to master your greed (and all that destructive self-criticism, too) by implementing some simple steps that you will learn along the way in a playful way.

Instead of being self-critical, learn to think the best of yourself!

Instead of being greedy, learn to think the best of others!

Sometimes it takes a little bit of time for someone to build confidence in this learning process, but I guarantee you if you follow the 5 easy steps of a system I will give you in a second, you will find both the confidence in and the results of this work. And you will find both really empowering!

So please don't be overly critical of yourself in this learning process. Go step by step and observe every little bit of progress you make. When you see advancements, celebrate them! And celebrate yourself. Critics do not celebrate themselves; they only hold themselves back and down. You can look up what is new and become experienced in following a simple 5-step "plan" - even if "plan" is a big word for something that about 8 billion people on earth should be doing as the most natural thing in the world.

THE 5-STEP SYSTEM:

1. *Be grateful!*
2. *Trust!*
3. *Be the one who feels best for yourself and who can have what you want to have.*
4. *Act as the one who feels great and who can have what you want to have.*
5. *Have what you want to have.*

Now you may ask me, what does this have to do with mastering greed?

I agree, at first glance, it is not obvious. But you just start with gratitude. That is the quickest way to not fall into the greed trap.

First of all, you will totally agree that greed is when you want more and more of something, even if you already have enough. Your constant gratitude diminishes that desire because you focus your attention on all the things you already have in your life instead of longing for the things you do not have. This is a completely different set of feelings. The idea of missing something has no place when you are full of love and gratitude for what you have. So, make a gratitude ritual your own, and own this wonderful feeling! It's best to do this every morning and every evening, and whenever you feel like it during the day. When it comes to the self-talk mentioned in the beginning, every time you observe yourself criticizing yourself, say instead: "My gratitude is greater than my expectations," and that alone will keep you in the right frequency.

You know that when you act in a greedy way, there can be consequences. One of those consequences is that you may be taking things away from others who also need or deserve them. If you truly feel gratitude for what you have, you will also transmit that to others. It is just natural that you would like to think that others will share this gratitude with you and that they will also feel good about what they have, which will make you less motivated to take from others. And with the level of gratitude you feel, you will also increase your level of confidence; you will somehow feel and believe that from the source of the things you already have, there will be even more things that you want to have in the future—without any need for greed, you will become more and more convinced that this is just a natural process. It flows!

My next point is that greed is born out of fear. Fear that there is not enough for you in a natural way. Fear that the things you have will be lost. Fear that you will come up short. So, you use the greed factor to push for more and more things to come into your life, even if it is completely irrelevant at the moment.

Did you know that most fears are completely unnecessary? Research and studies on fear and its necessity provide valuable insights into understanding the human psyche and how fear affects our lives. Fear, as a natural human emotion, can serve as a protective mechanism, but studies have proven that most of the fears we have today are a kind of legacy of humanity from times long ago when we were threatened by real dangers. Now you can sit in a wonderfully comfortable chair or on your sofa and think about losing your investment, and the fear kicks in instantly. You can think about that meeting with your boss—or your banker—in three days. Maybe you imagine that it will not be pleasant and you will get bad news, and as you sit there in that chair, you can feel pure panic even though there is no real threat.

It is just your fantasies about some event in the future.

There is no dangerous animal that is about to attack you or eat you up and smile, there is no one pointing a revolver at your forehead, but you feel fear. And it can be the same with your investments and finances. However, fear is worth noting when it is irrational or exaggerated and when it leads to anxiety about unlikely or improbable events. These irrational fears or phobias may stem from deep-seated psychological factors or traumatic experiences, but one thing is for sure: the reason for them is far less important than the effect that they can have. They can destroy your wealth if you allow fear to influence your decisions—and not just investment decisions.

And greed is the next plausible step when you are driven by fear. If there is fear, first become aware of the reason for that fear. Be warned: The fear is real; it is there in your entire body system. It is nothing more than a critical cocktail of hormones running through your veins. You can't imagine fear - it's definitely there - but get ahead of it by checking if the reason for your fear is really one that you should be allowing to run your hormone house. Maybe it is just a fantasy and it will never be a real fact in your life. Then get rid of the fear by feeling gratitude for all the beautiful things you have and the wonderful people around you!

Just a side note: You think your life is hard? You have so many problems? There is too little in your life to be truly grateful for? All the stress, the crisis, the inflation, the wars, the pandemics. Everything is bad! I wrote in the book *World Unlocked* that there are two million people out there—today!—who do not have a glass of fresh water.

"Most people reading this have also today urinated in toilets filled with fresh drinking water. That's right, your toilet is filled and refilled everyday with water just as clean as your water bottle. How many people in the world today don't have access to a single glass of fresh water to drink? THAT is a problem!" —*World Unlocked.* Written by Friends

You know, sometimes being greedy can cause problems in your relationships. People may not want to be friends with someone who is always greedy and doesn't think about other people's feelings. Remember that it is more important to be kind, share, and think about the needs of others than to always want more for yourself. And as a successful investor, you should cultivate a set of traits that are good for you because they are good for others. You should invest ethically, and you should also use your returns for the best possible benefit of all. That makes the returns plausible, and you can be much more relaxed because the source and the nature of all things is like that. Nature is abundant; there is no scarcity. In fact, scarcity is a consequence of fear, which leads to greed, which leads to scarcity of others. Your scarcity is the effect of the greed of others—not only for money, but much more for power. As soon as you know this, you may want to turn away from greed and get on the right path. Start with gratitude.

Wow, what a wonderful excursion into what I consider one of the most important topics for living in abundance, Gisi. Maybe the reader didn't expect this kind of information in a book about wealth protection and successful wealth creation. But believe me, dear reader, the most critical factor in your investment future is the state of mind and emotions you have as an investor. It is all about your decisions, because all the decisions you make will bring you good investments or bad compromises.

But I also want to emphasize an aspect that is really important. We all must learn to master greed for life. This is true for you, Gisi, for you, the reader, and certainly for me. Learning to master our greed can be one of the most challenging tasks in our lives.

Yes, Reto, greed is not easy to tame, but I believe it gets easier every time we put ourselves in the skin of another. Love is a big factor. If you feel love for the other person, not romantic love, I don't think I need to explain that, but if you really love the other person—your business partner, the clients who make an investment work, the people in the market, or those who serve for the success of any investment—as soon as you really feel love for them, you can't be that greedy.

DON'T TRY TO GET RICH AT SOMEONE ELSE'S EXPENSE
GET RICH BY TAKING RESPONSIBILITY

Don't try to make your wealth on the shoulders of others. Create wealth for as many others as possible!

In one of the houses, there was a family living there. They didn't pay the rent because the owner was unknown. They were just left there, and I just wanted to fix and flip the house. We had to kick them out even if they had to live on the street. So, I put my feelings on that issue aside because I just wanted the profit. Of course, things like this come back to you just like a boomerang, but it hits you harder than you can believe.

Yes, there are some decisions that pay off and others that you pay for. For sure! Similarly, as I said before, if you feel love for the people in a house (and I think you really could, even without knowing them; just imagine how it would feel to be in their shoes), you could probably own the house without them losing it.

You will find a solution for them to stay at home, and you will bring to light a situation in which literally everyone involved wins. It does not always have to be a win-win situation. The more you focus on more humane and ethical business and investment practices, the more win-win-win situations you will create.

The more people who win with what you are investing in, the more success you will enjoy! It could be so simple without greed.

I believe the purpose of any business is to solve problems for other people or other companies. What if we could rethink investing and create value in this way, and make the future itself our primary business purpose?

Let us make the future our business. Because if we don't, soon we won't have a business and we won't have a future. Let your first investment goal be to create value chains that benefit everyone. That is a completely different starting point than thinking about your own profit! And wait—please don't say "Hey, I'm not a charity" because I don't want you to become a charity. My point is success on different levels and in different dimensions: The more people involved who directly benefit from your investments, the more plausible and certain success becomes. The more YOU get back, and that is more than just more money!

Profit maximization can no longer be limited to classical profit. Profit is not only profit in the form of money. Profit is always WIN-WIN-WIN, and profit should be the value of life - winning for life. Profit can be safety and security. Profit must be awareness, health, and well-being!

Profit is the joy of life.

Profit should be natural regeneration, planting trees, and helping those who need help, while creating wealth for all involved. As soon as we all base our investment decisions on these fundamental ideas, the whole world—humanity—will come out of the state of fear and greed and live the way we were really born to live:

In true GREATNESS!

· ·

Oh, by the way, one of the things I do with my private mentoring clients is to challenge them to go for what they really want 100%. If YOU want to tell me what you really want, put this book away for a minute and drop my team a line via email at: exec@gisbertreuter.com

· ·

TALKING ABOUT
INFLATION

No, I don't want to waste your precious time talking about the problems of the world. You know them. But I think we should take a quick look behind the inflation that is eating away at your wealth right now: The cause of inflation is that more and more money is being printed. This means that more and more money is coming into the market without a corresponding increase in the amount of goods. This means that more and more money is coming onto the market, and in addition to the ratio to the quantity of goods, it is primarily the percentage of the total amount of your money on the market that determines whether inflation is a real problem for you. This is because the more money that is pumped into the market, the smaller the percentage of your money becomes. This means that your money is worth less and less. So, you pay more and more for the same goods or services. Because your money is worth less and less in this system, you need more and more money to get the same value in return. This is where things get really dizzy when you make investments that your banker has recommended to you because, for example, they yield a stable 4% or 6%. If the inflation rate is 10% (which you have been told is not true), then you are effectively losing 6% on such financial products, because even if you get 4%, the money is worth 10% less. So, you see, it's not only an interesting topic, but in this day and age where much of the world is totally fiat brainwashed, it's actually vital to study this topic and really learn how to protect yourself from inflation.

The good news first: It can be done. *The Swiss Wealth Creation* will show you how!

Let's also talk shortly about my small country: Switzerland. Why Switzerland? Switzerland's neutrality has given it a unique position for centuries. This means that it is in the middle of Europe, has connections everywhere, and yet is neutral. Switzerland is independent of other countries and has always been considered a safe haven for a lot of capital. Switzerland does not have many natural resources. But what the Swiss do have is a lot of knowledge, and that includes a lot of banking knowledge. Switzerland is very well known around the world as a financial center because it has a very stable currency. In fact, Switzerland has done a better job of controlling inflation than almost any other country in the world. Whatever crises are going on in the world, Switzerland's neutrality means that we are not involved in any wars. And since we have no raw materials—other than marmots and edelweiss, fresh alpine milk, and chocolate with purple cows—we really do focus 100 percent on our services. And that's where we, undisputedly, are number one in the world.

As far as the inflation hedge is concerned, the decisive factor is that inflation in Switzerland is very well under control. What this means for you is that if you invest the same amount of money in Switzerland, it will retain its value more securely and to a higher degree than anywhere else in the world. That's why wealth preservation in Switzerland is extremely good, extremely stable, extremely sustainable, and extremely efficient. This is why so many of the world's leading companies are based in Switzerland. In addition to the tax advantages, it is clearly the security factor. Security and trust are written in capital letters in Switzerland. Switzerland has been an international financial center for decades. Even though banking secrecy is not as strict as it used to be, it still makes sense for many people around the world to invest their money in Switzerland. The Swiss government is also known for having very little influence on financial assets. In other words, unlike in Europe and other countries around the world, the government does not have access to investors' assets! It has no legal means of accessing assets that are in Swiss hands. Switzerland is also unique in that it has many duty-free warehouses, some of which are located in the airport area, as is the case in many other countries, but there are also many that are located directly in the Swiss Alps and are highly secure, far away from major public transportation routes, so that no one can easily access them.

From an eagle's perspective, these are some of the characteristic advantages that Switzerland has built up over decades and centuries. Together with its neutrality, this means that Switzerland is considered *the* safe haven for assets that can be stored here in Switzerland, where access is secure, and which can also be brought into the profit zone much more quickly thanks to low inflation. This means that assets can even grow extraordinarily. The Swiss cross continues to enjoy a very high international reputation among those seeking trust and security.

Amazing! I am really looking forward to creating this book with you, Reto, and I am happy to get to know all your expertise and thoughts on the subject. I love Switzerland, and did you know that there is even a village named after me? Gisikon! But that is another story… I had some thoughts earlier when you told us about learning how to handle greed (yes, this is kind of an afterburner, but I think it is too important to let go) that I want to come back to: Now that we are both in a long-term mentoring relationship that I really enjoy, do you think that if you had a great mentor at the time of your first 100% ROI, that mentor would have prevented you from losing money? What do you think?

Oh yes, of course! Mentorship is a really big factor because when you have been raised since you were a little kid to think that 6% is fine but 100% ROI is insane, of course you go totally crazy when you get those kinds of results for the first time. Of course you want to go further, and of course you want more and more and more, and of course, you're kind of blind to the other side of the coin. You need somebody who has a broader perspective, who has been there. So, yeah, I really believe in mentorship because it is one of the most important and efficient tools you can have to get systematic support.

Not just the network and the community, or someone who has been there and experienced it like you have, but someone who has ten or twenty years more experience with situations that you are just going through for the first time. A great mentor is priceless. A great mentor gives you 20 years of learning. And a great mentor can do that in just six months. For me at that time, it definitely would have saved me from getting into the nightmare and losing hundreds of thousands, not to mention I would have done less harm to people who were depending on me. I still feel bad about the bad decisions I made back then. How I wish I had had a great mentor, but I did not. We will come back to this amazing topic later.

WHEN
ONE SETBACK
IS NOT ENOUGH

In 2016 and 2017, I did a lot of crypto projects. I knew that many of these projects were not serious. I knew that many of them were pyramid schemes and I accepted that. I got into a few systems that paid really well. At the same time, bitcoin was going up pretty fast. So, I quit my job because I had three systems that were paying me on a regular basis. And they were paying very well. I could make a decent living off of it.

If I had only truly learned my lesson back then, but I still had no idea how to manage my greed. So, I cashed out my pension plan and put it all into bitcoin. At that time, I just knew it was the greatest thing to do because bitcoin was going through the roof. I knew I was going to make a lot of money and I wouldn't have to worry about finances anymore. It was two months later that all three of these systems collapsed.

There was no money coming in. On top of that, bitcoin prices started to fall, so the value of my assets started to fall. And every month when I had to take out money to live, I had to take out more bitcoin than the previous month. I could see my assets just shrinking towards the zero level. I could already see the zero level and I knew that something had to change or I would go straight to bankruptcy. I couldn't sleep at night. I woke up with sweat on my forehead. I didn't know how I was going to get through the next day. And the worst part was that the people around me didn't know how bad it really was.

I didn't have the courage to tell the truth. I felt like the worst failure on the face of the earth. I even had a cruise planned with my wife that cost a fortune and I was broke. We didn't know how to pay for it. My whole house fell apart. My wife and I got sick right before we were supposed to go on the trip, so we were able to cancel the trip and get the money back from the insurance.

That was kind of a sign for me. I finally decided to get another job to at least have my stable monthly income again. And then I started to fill in the holes in my bank account, and my credit cards, so I got out of my personal debt. Sometimes you have to go through some lessons twice. Surely a great mentor would have been able to avoid both of these episodes of greed.

GET
SMART
QUICK

Okay, let's face it: You've been told your whole life to "save your money and be careful with your investments".

What they didn't tell you is that you should be doing this so that someone else who knows better—aka the banker—can invest your hard-earned money in various assets. Most of the time they were anything but careful with your money; at best, they invested in real assets like their luxury buildings. But I bet you remember the subprime mortgage crisis, and I think you would be very surprised if you took a day or two to really investigate where the big banks are investing their money.

So let me be clear. You have been told lies for most of your life: You've been told that you need a bank as a link between storing value and paying with your money. That's a myth! Here's why…

YOU DON'T NEED A BANK
YOU NEED BANKING

If you want the ability to store value in a safe and secure way and to transfer money from one place to another, there are a number of options, but all of these alternatives mean that you face significant challenges.

Most of them are in your subconscious.

It took a lifetime to plant them there, but since they are programs that are now running, we need to reprogram them so that you can change your investment habits and get much better results for your life.

Ask yourself: How sure is your bank when it comes to returns?

Do they always get it right? From experience, no, they don't. For instance, when you are having a conversation with the banker and ask, "How are you personally invested? Do you have exactly these products that you want to sell me here?" Then it usually gets very quiet! The banker then tries to make excuses and you realize that what he is trying to sell you is not something he has invested in himself. And that is an absolute no-go for me because it simply tells you that the banker is selling you products that have been ordered from above, products that bring the bank the most fees, products that they want to push; be it for political or internal reasons, they simply have to make sales figures now. But if the banker himself is not invested in these products, why should I, as a customer, invest in them?

Reto, you are so right. For me, there is even another point that I think every reader should be aware of. Why don't you go, dear reader, and open Google on your browser and type in "average salary of a bank employee"?

> I just copied the first number at random: "The average banking salary in the U.S. is $67,329 per year, or $32.37 per hour." (https://www.talent.com/salary?job=banking). Oh, you want to know the German equivalent: "Bank Employee salary in Germany—2023. Monthly Median Gross Salary 5,235.00€ (equals 62,820.00€ per year) based on 228,525 salaries" (https://lohntastik.de). Let's skip all other countries; do you really think that someone with that kind of salary should be someone you listen to when it comes to how to get very rich? I don't think so! If it is your idea to become a millionaire, you should ask someone who was once in a similar situation to the one you are in now, and who is now a millionaire and has been for at least 10, or even better, 20 years.

If you want to become a wealthy investor, ask someone who has not always been a successful investor, but who has learned how to get from where you are to where you want to be. It is just as important that the person you ask understands your current situation as it is, and that he or she knows how to get there, and how to reach the goals you want to achieve. Both points - your starting point and your destination - are of exactly the same fundamental importance.

Have you ever tried to program your GPS without knowing where you are? Without knowing your location, it's impossible. So, the advisor you choose must know what it is like to be in your shoes, and he must be experienced in creating value through wise investing habits.

And if you want to know how to overcome the fear of breaking new ground, ask someone who has walked new paths many times in his own life and, at best, also guided many—many(!)—others through their transformation processes. And believe me, going from being a loyal bank customer to being an independent, successful investor is quite a rodeo! It is not something you can do by reading a book. However, it is true that, as you read the right books, you already have a huge advantage that sets you apart from millions of others out there who would never get a book like this in their hands.

But there are more aspects to this topic when we ask how well banks are managing plausible returns. For example, it is sad but true that funds for digital health experienced a decline of 60 percent during the last few years. Because of the pandemic and, with it, the ongoing digitalization of the healthcare system and the high demand for companies involved in this transformation, investments in digital health have been steadily increasing over the years, and the long-term prospects for this industry remain promising. But even though companies involved in digitizing healthcare have full order books until 2028, the bank product shows a tight -60% performance.

So, Reto, I think it is of unparalleled importance for our readers to make up their minds, especially about the lies they have been told all their lives. You and I and the reader—we have all been told this nonsense and it is time to rethink what we have been programmed to believe about banks.

YOUR BANK IS INTERESTED IN YOUR WEALTH

No, it isn't. The assumption that the bank is remotely interested in your profit is false. The only interest a bank has is that you believe the banker knows something you don't. And that knowledge is so complicated—after all, it's your money—that you won't be able to learn that secret wisdom. Just hand over this heavy responsibility to your banks so they can handle your money and charge you tons of fees. That is what the bank really wants!

YOUR BANK KNOWS WHAT IT IS DOING

It is also wrong to assume that the bank or its asset management department knows what it is doing. That's the reason for every banking crisis that has ever happened and will ever happen. So, let's get this topic check marked: You don't need a bank, you need banking. And you can learn everything you need to know and do to become a successful investor! But there are some more myths we definitely want to get out of your way first. Reto, what are some of the arguments you hear over and over again from people who are at the beginning of this transition from being a subordinate bank client to becoming a self-confident, successful investor? One of the most common things I hear is: I don't know where to invest. And it is all about feeling safe with your investment decisions.

ABOUT FEEL-GOOD PERCENTAGES

Many people just don't know where to invest, so they stay with their bank. You just learned the wise answer to the second part of this statement, so let us focus on where to get good information for your investments. Before we go into some very detailed information about great *Swiss Wealth Creation* investments in the second part of the book, I just want you to open your mind for now.

For you at this point, the most important question is always: "How is the value created?" So when I see a product that piques my interest, my first question is always, where does that interest come from? What is the whole added value behind the product?

If a piece of clothing is made in China for ten dollars and then sold here for 50 francs, then 40 francs of added value has simply been generated on the market by a commercial product, and that is very plausible to me.

— Let me interrupt you, Reto, because this brings another example to my mind I love to use when I wish to open someone's eyes related to high-risk yields.

I imagine that you, dear reader, are one of those who believe that returns above 10% must be high-risk investments. If that is the case, pay some extra attention now.

You want to get a general idea of how much higher returns can be than you think are possible with zero risk. Let me give you a very simple example: Water!

How much does a 1-liter bottle of water cost? "That depends," you might answer. "You mean Perrier? Acqua di Cristallo? Tap water?"—Yes, the "brand" is a big factor. But it also depends on where you buy it.

While in a restaurant, you can be charged 8 dollars/ francs or euros for the same bottle that you get for 1.20 at the grocery store, or 4.95 at the gas station. So here alone you have a margin of 1.20 to 8.00. That's a solid 7.20 markup; that's 600%! Do you think it is riskier for someone to sell water in a restaurant than in a grocery store? To open your mind, just remember: 600%—six hundred percent and ZERO risk!

> But you are welcome to go one step further with me: A cubic meter of water costs on average between €1.20 and €2.00. Water prices are usually set by local authorities. So you can buy a 1-liter bottle of water at your local supermarket for 1.20, or you can get a cubic meter of water from your local municipality for the same price. Now, do you know how many liters are in one cubic meter of water? 1 cubic meter = 1,000 liters. If you can get 1000 liters for 1.20 and you bottle it, you can get a 100,000% return. Where is the risk of high yield now? You just have to do it.

And when it comes to tales, such as the one that claims high yields must be very volatile and risky investments, let me share this one I'm sure everyone is familiar with:

Once upon a time, a smart student and a few of his friends made a website called TheFacebook. It was a special website that helped people connect with each other at colleges. You could find people from your school, see who is in your classes, and even see who your friends'

friends are. At first, it was only for Harvard students, but then it became popular and spread to other colleges too.

By the end of 2004, TheFacebook had more than 1 million users! It was so successful that they moved the company to Silicon Valley and got a big investment of $500,000. They changed the name to just "Facebook" in 2005 and opened it to everyone in 2006. That's when it really started to grow.

Just a side note: one of my friends and business partners invested 250.000 euro back in 2006 in this company. But before being able to send the wire transfer, the director of a very well-known German Bank was calling him "totally nuts". "Are you crazy?" he said. "Don't do that. How can you even think of putting your money in that kind of company?"

In just three years, Facebook had 350 million users! Can you believe it? And in 2012, it became the first website to have 1 billion people using it every month. That's a lot of people! By the end of 2018, there were 2.32 billion people using Facebook. That means more than half of the people who use the internet are on Facebook.

It's amazing how a teenager's idea turned into such a big and popular website, but the moral of the story is that returns of several thousand percent are certainly possible. Of course, these are exceptions, and a bit of luck is definitely involved, but as long as you think that anything over 10% is either a rip-off or very risky, you're only standing in your own way and will NEVER use gems like this for yourself. Just like the bank manager who tried to stop my friend and partner from doing so, you will believe this is only for stupid idiots, while some of them are making billions with it!

So, Reto, what is it that you want to know from a company before you consider investing your own money in it?

If I invest directly in a company, of course, I know that when the company generates more sales and the net profit increases, a dividend can be paid out of that net profit. Those things are plausible to me, but you have to look at the whole value chain. We come back to this very important topic of value chains later in this book.

For now, it is vital that we are on the same page about feel-good percentages. And most people have had it hammered into them for their entire lives that 2, 3, or 4 percent is a good and solid return. You should understand right now that this 2, 3 or 4 percent that is generated somewhere is often a small part of the total profit generated—as long as you don't know the rules of the game or learn them—and the biggest cut is for others.

You can definitely change this now.

Start with opening your mind.

BE
YOUR OWN
BANK

When you see how much profit a bank makes and how much interest you get as the customer, then you know for sure that the bank takes your money, works with it, and makes a profit with it, then pays you just a small contribution. If that! My tip for you: go straight into the market and look at the bank as the middleman. Let the bank be your tool. Again: You don't need a bank, you need banking!

Let's have a look at how banks work: Cembra Money Bank offers medium-term bonds at around 2% per year. If you bought a Cembra Money Share at the end of 2021 for CHF 65, then you received a dividend of CHF 3.95 which equals 6%; this is 300% more ROI by just knowing what to buy.

So, do not subordinate yourself. Don't accept anyone that takes the biggest profit for themselves and only gives you a small portion of the money. Go and take the bigger piece of the pie for yourself. Be your own bank!

That is so true, Reto, and just as a side story: I am working with some contacts who themselves have mandates to look for some banks to buy. But you know, the wonderful thing is that you don't have to be a member of the ultra-high net worth club—or in other words, you don't have to be one of those people with a net worth of at least $30 million in investable assets-to own your own bank. Read what Reto says: there is a difference between owning your own bank and being your Own Bank. Just BE! Even if you are only thinking of investing 10,000 or less of your hard-earned money, there are several very plausible solutions and real opportunities for you to BE your own bank. If you want to know how, read carefully what Reto and I share on the last page of this book and let us connect. Because: Connection is the new currency.

OH! YOU HAVE NO MONEY TO INVEST?

There may be some myths, stories, and hard-coded lies in your mind, and I want to spend a few moments addressing these phantoms because if we don't, they could easily hold you back from getting very rich. The first and most dangerous is the belief that most people have. Do you think you have no money to invest?

It can stem from several factors. One primary reason is the perception that investing requires a large sum of money upfront. Many people I was in contact with believe that they need significant amounts of disposable income to start investing, which can create a barrier to entry. Additionally, people's financial circumstances and priorities vary. Some individuals may have limited income due to low wages or financial obligations, such as debt or high living expenses. These factors can make it challenging for you to allocate some funds for investment purposes.

Perhaps there is a lack of financial literacy and awareness about the benefits of investing. Many people may not fully understand the potential long-term advantages of investing and how it can contribute to financial independence.

Anyway, the belief that you have no money to invest can hold you back from becoming financially independent because investing is a crucial component of wealth accumulation. By not investing, you miss out on the opportunity to grow your wealth and potentially achieve financial freedom in the long run. Let me get to the point: "I have no money to invest" is a lie. Maybe the jeans you're wearing were expensive enough to take a small but meaningful first step into your investing future. Who knows - the shoes in your closet may have cost many times more than what it takes to get started as an investor.

Did you know that one domino can topple another domino that is 1.6 times bigger than the first?

Did you know exactly when your capital doubles if you only achieve 1% growth every day? After only 70 days, you have doubled your capital. That is, if we stay with your jeans. Let them cost 70€ "Levi's 501 Original Fit" and let's take this 70€ as your starting capital for this example.

After 70 days, this is 140€ and you're still thinking "no big deal", but stay with me: after 350 days, i.e., in just one year, this amount would have grown to a mini extra fortune of 2.240€. After about three years (if you want to know exactly after 980 days), it would be **1.146.880€**

One million one hundred forty-six thousand eight hundred eighty Euro.

So, now: Do you still think you don't have enough to start being a successful investor?

This is a lie!

The truth is: It is important for you to know that even very small amounts of money can be invested and have a significant impact on your wealth over time. By busting the myth that investing requires large sums of money, you can begin to explore investment options and take steps toward financial independence.

Just as a second example:

Let's replace the $70 with $10,000, an amount I believe most people can truly invest in their future.

Now look at the math on the following little chart.

Days	Amount	490	1.280.000,00 €
0	10.000,00 €	560	2.560.000,00 €
70	20.000,00 €	630	5.120.000,00 €
140	40.000,00 €	700	10.240.000,00 €
210	80.000,00 €	770	20.480.000,00 €
280	160.000,00 €	840	40.960.000,00 €
350	320.000,00 €	910	81.920.000,00 €
420	640.000,00 €	980	163.840.000,00 €

Wouldn't it be much smarter to ask, "How can I get 1% growth a day" instead of lying to yourself and talking yourself out of that wonderful future by saying you don't have any money to invest? But there is another trap. You might think...

YOU NEED TO PAY YOUR MORTGAGE FIRST?

No, you don't. Yes, this is a typical Swiss belief: Pay off the mortgage first, then you can live almost for free and have enough money to live on in old age. Without financial education and a willingness to take personal responsibility, this approach is certainly correct. But what do the successful do? They often borrow as much as they can, with good credit, so that they have enough money to invest in other investment opportunities.

These are often interest-differential deals: if I pay 5% interest and principal and can invest my money for 15%, I have 10% left over! If I have a 100,000 loan and pay 5,000 for it, but invest the 100,000 at 15%, I get 15,000. After deducting the 5,000, I am left with 10,000! Robert Kiyosaki keeps saying that your house is a liability, not an asset: your house takes money out of your pocket every month (interest, amortization, repairs, ...).

You can change this if you have a studio or a second home in your house that you can rent out and that brings you money every month. If the rental income is higher than the interest and amortization, then you have a positive cash flow, and your house becomes an asset!

I take this one step further. Let's say I buy a house for 1 million and have to bring 200,000 equity and pay 5% interest and amortization, then that's 40,000 interest and amortization per year (3,333.33 per month). If I don't buy the house and invest the 200,000 equity at 15%, I get a return of 30,000 per year (2,500 per month). This means that if I rent another 2,500, I have an additional 3,333.33 in my cash that I don't have to spend, for a total of 5,833.33 per month. For 3,000 a month, I can rent a great apartment in Switzerland and have an extra 2,833.33 to spend!

And if things get tight, I can always rent a cheaper apartment. If owning your own home is a dream and you don't want to give it up, then at least have a high mortgage and let the disposable money work for you so you can build your wealth much faster and higher in the long run.

IF IT WERE THAT SIMPLE EVERYONE WOULD DO IT!

Do you know that smoking is unhealthy? I know you do! So, let me ask you - why are there still people who smoke? The human psyche is often incomprehensible. Many things happen that cannot be explained logically, and it's the same with money. For decades, we have been taught that we should save, and that the higher the return, the higher the risk. This isn't true! Of course there are some dependencies, but one of the biggest risks is when someone has too much money in their bank account! And now opportunities are coming your way that are too good to be true. A 10% investment opportunity.

All the red lights are on. I didn't learn about it, I haven't seen any advertisements for it, and it has never been mentioned on TV except in one report where someone got ripped off and lost everything. All I have to do is register and from now on I can buy silver and gold in the bonded warehouse? That sounds too easy.

What if ... the average increase in value is higher than or equal to inflation? Yes, but ... I prefer to ask my banker and my neighbor; they know a lot about such topics. And I often wonder what else my counterpart needs to see the obvious, acknowledge it, and be willing to implement it. It's so simple, most investment opportunities can be done in a very short time, and it's often easier than opening a bank account. The returns are many times what the bank pays, yet not everyone does it.

WE LIVE IN UNCERTAIN TIMES — IT'S BETTER TO WAIT AND SEE WHAT'S COMING BEFORE MAKING ANY INVESTMENT DECISIONS NOW...

I repeat deliberately: The world is undergoing the biggest change ever! And most of the world's current businesses do not meet the demands and needs of the times. Linear thinking meets exponential reality. Too many business leaders are not thinking about the social component. The main problem with global leadership is the clumsy, awkward, slow, and graceless approach of governments.

We don't see any government on earth that has the entrepreneurial mindset. There is no commitment beyond the next election. There is no agility at all! Politicians are the last people on earth willing to take risks. This means that the world's problems cannot be solved by governments. But the world needs saviors!

The world's problems can be solved, without exception, by solid, healthy, and thoughtful businesses. Now ask yourself one simple question: why not yours?

Gisi, I love that statement! As soon as one says, "we are in challenging times, it's better to wait and see what's coming", you see how easy it is to abdicate responsibility, be it to the uncertain future, to the banker, or to simply do nothing at all.

We will always have uncertain times. One characteristic of the future is that it hasn't happened yet, so we don't know what will happen. This has always been the case and will always remain so. And what is certain is that the future will happen! Why are so many people reluctant to take the next step? Is it the uncertainty as to whether they are doing the right thing? Or whether it will actually turn out well? In my opinion, over 80% of people don't want to take responsibility! Responsibility for their money, for their own lives, and for their decisions! For most people, it's much better and more comfortable if someone tells them what to do. Then it will be right, and if not, then they have a scapegoat. Our economy and politics know how to exploit this. With a lot of advertising and propaganda, you can influence people and guide them to do and say what you want them to do and say. It is always frightening to me how the press can control which topics are discussed in the break rooms. And if they want to divert focus from something, another topic is pushed to the fore and only that one is reported on. And within 24 to 48 hours, an entire population is only talking about this topic. I don't want to get political here, but I am aware of how often manipulation takes place. And bad and insecure reports also discourage most of the population from taking responsibility for their own finances. They prefer to wait and see what the future brings, and then they can still get involved if need be. If I have an investment opportunity on the table, then I check it out, and if I am convinced that it fits in with my investment strategy, then I close it!

Of course, I also look at what is happening both globally and locally, and whether and how this could have an impact on the investment opportunity. If this is minimal, then nothing should stand in the way, especially when it comes to tangible assets: no matter what happens in the economy and in the world, I still have the tangible asset in my hand. A kilo of silver remains a kilo of silver, whether there is a flood, immigration, or climate change. Even if the future is uncertain, my kilo of silver retains its value, so I can buy it today.

Yes, Reto, I totally agree, and there is even more to this topic than precious metals and other assets that are in everyone's hands to create wealth. There is another issue of immeasurable importance. Every now and then, you are fortunate enough to raise your standard of living.

Your life, your lifestyle, your quality of life, to a whole new level. It was in the 15th century when the "Gutenberg Revolution" and the age of printed books had a tremendous impact on the knowledge of all future generations.

Fast-forwarding beyond automobiles, manned aviation, and electricity—there are three other categories that have changed everything: the telephone, the Internet, and your smartphone.

Today we share the moment of the next category creation: The category of our time, and this category is about *sourcing our future!* We are in a time that brings an unprecedented opportunity to create a lasting legacy with the priceless achievements of human history. The current economic, social, and technological climate are now creating the optimal conditions for humanity to make this pivotal turn in our future—seize it now!

We must come together to take full advantage of this time. And if we do, these uncertain times are the opportunity of your lifetime (as it is the opportunity of my lifetime!) This is the certainty I can give you in uncertain times: Connection is the new currency! So, let's connect and do good together, and the rest of this book will show you several ways to do just that.

PART II

MASTERING YOUR ART OF INVESTMENT

THE TRUST FACTOR:
YOUR KEY TO THRIVING IN UNCERTAIN TIMES

NOW: Get ready to receive actual investment principles directly from the center of the world's trust—that is, Switzerland—to not only use The Swiss Wealth Creation as a wealth protection aid, but to create exponential results in your portfolio.

In this chapter, we'll cover it all, including the key to your wealth, money for freedom, gold and silver, digital currencies, preserving your value, accumulating wealth, cash flow projects, and much more.

Attention: If you are short on time, you can use the "speed read" sections at the top of each chapter to find the topic that will be most helpful to you. Often, you will find that these quick summaries will be of great value in helping you make your next important decision. Later, you can go

deeper into the details and complete your treasure trove of The Swiss Wealth Creation knowledge.

The following system for your investments is a system I use myself, and I want to be completely transparent: I did not invent it. It is not important to invent something new when you can use systems that have already made billions for others. So, I am standing on the shoulders of giants—truly incredible investors that I have learned from, and I am happy to share with you the most important takeaways of all the teachings that I have been blessed to receive. I will organize the following teaching points into 5 major categories or modules.

1 — Cash Reserves

2 — Asset Protection

3 — Asset Accumulation

4 — Cash Flow Projects

5 — Real Estate

You will see that each module has several sub-chapters, which are possibilities to realize plausible growth of your wealth as well as its protection.

THE POWER OF CASH RESERVES: BUILDING YOUR FINANCIAL FUTURE

Speed Read: Always have some cash available for deals coming around the corner.

- *The reserve—it gives you a lot of security.*
- *You have a good feeling because you know you have your reserve.*
- *Come what may, it will improve your overall appearance and therefore your impact and all your results—not just financial.*

The first thing to do is to build up your reserve because that will give you a lot of security no matter what happens, whether it's something small, like a doctor's bill, or something big, like your car breaks down and you have to buy a new one. If you don't have a cash reserve, you're always thinking about money, and always thinking in terms of lack! Your reserve dissolves all this lack thinking, and the positive results will go far beyond your financial successes.

As long as you are in this scarcity mindset, you are not allowing the source of everything, call it "the universe", call it "God", call it "life"—the term ultimately doesn't matter—to give you more. There will be nothing but lack if you think lack.

Because then your life will only ever be about filling the holes. It will always be about putting out fires, and believe me, a well-built poverty consciousness, which most of us have inherited from others, will always bring enough fires into your life that it will be difficult to get out of it. So, you are well advised to work on your thoughts to make these reserves possible. If you want to know how to approach subconscious programming and how to reprogram your subconscious to allow better thoughts in the long run, then contact Gisi. There is no one on earth who can help you better in taking a quantum leap breakthrough with your programming. But let us stay on the subject of cash reserves here.

Therefore, understanding that a lot comes from your good feelings is extremely important to becoming a successful investor! That you really know that you have your reserves, come what may! And this will also boost your external appearance enormously. You will gain much more power, and experience effectiveness.

Without effort, whether in your job, in negotiations with your banker, or with your friends, if you simply know that you have enough security behind you; for example, that you can live well for three to six months without income and easily cover your expenses.

But there's another important point that speaks in favor of your reserve: when an opportunity comes along—and believe me, once you're ready to accept these opportunities, they will come to you in such an overwhelming way that you won't have to do anything but be prepared—so, when an opportunity comes along that you rarely have and that you've checked for yourself as being a perfect fit, then you can also take advantage of that opportunity. And you'll be able to take advantage of it without having to worry about how you're going to finance it now, without having to worry about where you're going to get a certain amount of money quickly, or how you're going to fund that investment to take advantage of that opportunity, because you have your reserve that you can use to grow your portfolio accordingly.

And when I think about what's going on in the financial industry right now, when I think about what could be coming, I know there are some really, really great opportunities ahead of us, and when you are mentally prepared and well positioned in terms of your reserves, you're going to benefit across the board, just like the best investors did during the financial crisis in 2008 and

2009. You may also know that, in recent years, despite the pandemic, despite the crises, despite the drastic economic imbalance, more new trillionaires have been created in the world than ever before, so the question is not whether it is possible to create enormous wealth even in very difficult times. The question is, is it possible for you, too? The answer is a resounding yes. In the next nine chapters, we will show you how.

I already look forward to all these chapters, Reto, and to the fact that I will learn so much from you. By the way, did you know that you are a perfect example of the Law of Resonance (what others call the "Law of Attraction")? I really mean that, Reto. You are a priceless treasure, and you have priceless treasures to bestow as an investor and advisor.

So, if we take another look at the 5 steps that we talked about in the chapter on greed and mastering it, those steps 3 to 5 are actually the key essence of this law: be—do—have, or as I said: Be the one who feels best and can have what you want. Act as the one who feels great and can have what you want to have. Have what you want to have.

You are the treasure you want to have, and you are definitely the best treasure as a counselor empowering others to have what they want to have—so you are a perfect example of the Law of Resonance!

That said, I really can't wait to experience the next chapters with you and implement what you share, with alacrity! Just as a side: It is an absolute honor and pleasure to write this book with you.

To you, the reader: if you ever have a chance to work with Reto, do it; he will change your life! He changed mine!

Let's start with how we build our reserves. I know this question very well because I know how it feels when you think you don't have the means to really set aside an amount of money that will serve you when you need it. How can the reader build the kind of wealth cushion you talk about when each month's income is barely enough to cover living expenses?

Well, Gisi, what I see again and again today is that phenomenon: the more you earn, the more you spend. And if you have the awareness that when you will receive 200 francs more - let's say next month as a salary increase - that you don't just increase your expenses by 200 Swiss francs, but that, ideally, you can put the whole 200 francs on the side and invest it month by month, and so on. Then you can also manage to build up your cash reserve, and at the same time, you reduce your awareness of expenses more and more.

Another point is to really list every expense in detail for a month and then analyze where your money actually goes. How much do you spend every day on stuff that is not financially necessary? Why do you—just as a simple example—buy a liter of water at the gas station for four or five francs when you can get the same liter for 50 centimes at the supermarket? And when you keep putting these small amounts aside, you'll be amazed at how much money you end up with. Every evening, when I have spare change in my pocket, it all goes into a pot so that I go out again every new day and I only have one coin. I take what I need for shopping, or for the trolley, and all the other change goes into the reserve. There's also a lot of change. Just try it out for six months.

I love the simplicity of your tips and how suitable they are for everyday use, Reto! Dear reader, don't make a mistake now by becoming a penny-pincher. That's not what Reto is all about.

Oh, of course not—no! You may be familiar with the famous Wage Poem by Jesse B. Rittenhouse:

"I bargained with Life for a penny,
and Life would pay no more,
However I begged at evening
When I counted my scanty store;
Life is a just employer.
He gives you what you ask,
But once you have set the wages,
Why, you must bear the task.
I worked for a menial's hire,
Only to learn, dismayed,
That any wage I had asked of Life,
Life would have willingly paid."

Be aware that putting away pennies is only for the cushion; this cushion is like the first lead domino of your wealth creation.

I just want to explain to you how you can easily save a considerable amount of money in your everyday life with very simple means that are guaranteed to be available, without major losses! Think of pennies to build up a reserve and think BIG about what this reserve can be in 5 to 10 years.

But let us start small: Can you imagine putting away 200 francs —every time I say francs, feel free to substitute "dollars" or "euros"— and would you like to know how those 200 francs could grow in just 17 months from now?

Imagine that at the end of the month you can have 200 francs in this cushion-lead domino.

Now you need to know—and read these next lines very carefully—that each domino block can knock over a next domino that is about 1.6 times larger. We play it through:

> 200 x 1.6 = 320 x 1.6 = 512 x 1.6 = 819 x 1.6 = 1,320 x 1.6 = 2,097 x 1.6 = 3,355 x 1.6 = 5,369 x 1.6 = 8,590 x 1.6 = 13,744 x 1.6 = 21,990 x 1.6 = 35,184 x 1.6 = 56,295 x 1.6 = 90,072 x 1.6 = 144,115 x 1.6 = 230,584 x 1.6 = 368,935 x 1.6 = 590,295.

This is 17 "domino blocks" or 17 months of building your cash reserve based on 200 francs, euros, or dollars you put away.

How will it feel to have $590,000 (Euro or CHF) at your back without having to work hard for it?

Let us play this example a little bit more: $2,417,851 (Euro or CHF) will be the result of "just three domino blocks" more. Now you know why it is so important to have that cash reserve, even when I did not mention that. On your way to growing your wealth, there is plenty of room to put away an amount that always guarantees that you could go through a 3 or 6-month period without earnings. Just imagine taking 50K out of this domino chain and having it for emergencies.

So, now: Do you want to learn how to make a 1,6 X growth with your cash reserve?

The good news: you definitely can do that!

In the following chapters you will find several ways to do this.

GOLD BANKING FOR FREEDOM WITH **MONEY FOR FREEDOM!**

Speed Read:

There are several emerging systems and protocols around the world that support global payments with real gold and silver. There are also numerous Swiss companies with a common denominator: To bring back the gold standard to the world. That means gold as a payment system and/or a gold-backed currency. And in some very special endeavors, this idea is linked to the creation of a much more humane economy—we believe this is the noblest endeavor of our time.

That's why we—the authors—are currently working on a vision and a project that rethinks money and banking, and we aim to position ourselves as a Category of One beyond fiat money. And there's more: We plan to go far beyond today's old crypto, making fiat obsolete and old crypto look like a BlackBerry the moment the iPhone hits the stage!

I wish the battle against CBDCs was not already lost, but it seems it is. Even so, you can help. That is why this chapter is special in this book. When we talk about gold and what gold means to you as an inflation hedge, we also want to draw your attention to what gold means to you compared to fiat, CBDCs, or even all the crypto alternatives. So let us go on a golden journey!

Once you have your liquidity reserve, you should continue to put money away on average every month, ideally through a savings plan. It can be a savings plan in precious metals - in strategic metals. It can be a savings plan in gold and silver, and ideally you can execute that plan with a tap of your finger on your mobile device.

Yes, Reto, we are in a time that supports wealth creation like no other. But even if we were to go back decades or centuries, there is one factor about gold that I want to emphasize before we dive deep into the modern solutions we have at our disposal today. So first, some universal facts about gold:

THE GOLD PRICE IS STABLE

There are people out there who say that the price of gold has been going up for the last 100 years. In fact, if you look at the following charts, you can see that the price of gold has in fact risen an average of about 7% to 8% per year. Yes, there have been down years. But the point I want to make is this. Don't let such statements mislead you into misunderstanding an essential factor. *It is not the case that the value of gold goes up or down.* What you are really seeing in these charts is the fiat currency dollar losing or gaining confidence.

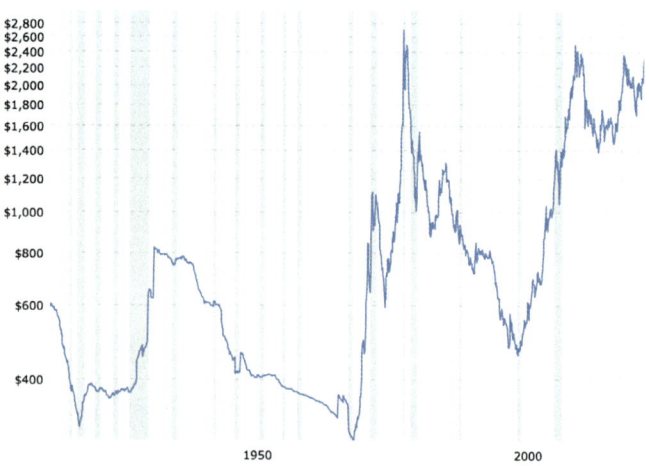

Historical gold prices: 100-year-chart (April, 2024)

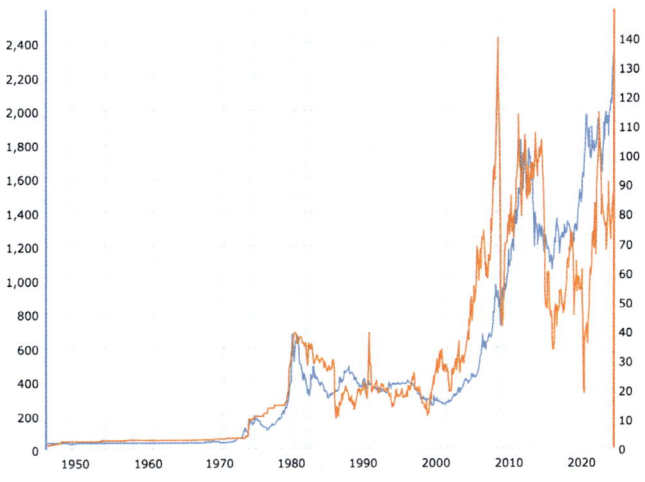

Historical gold prices: gold vs oil (April, 2024)

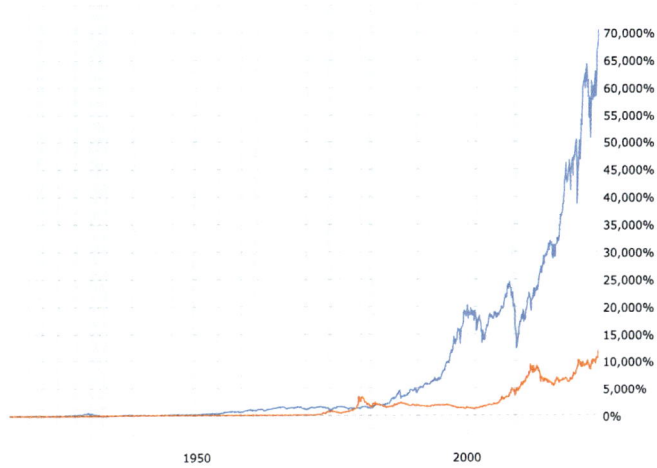

Historical gold prices: gold vs stock market (April, 2024)

So, from now on, remember: when "the price of gold goes up," it really means that the dollar is worth less. And when "the price of gold goes down" it means that more people are gaining confidence in the dollar again, which really means that the powers behind it have done a good job of accomplishing their fiat brainwashing. If you are betting your future on gold, there are several very promising factors that will support your wealth building.

1. With gold, you own the most accepted commodity on earth. Wherever you go with a few gold coins, you will get a service or product for them, even in extreme situations.
2. You own a value that rises in price when the world loses faith in paper money.
3. You own a value that will not go down even if the world thinks that paper with funny pictures on it is a good idea. You can play the fiat game to a certain extent without problems and your gold is just there in the back to get you through the next time of trouble.
4. We are in a time of trouble. So gold is the thing to own right now.
5. And the most important fact of all. A kilo of gold will still be a kilo of gold in a thousand years, and it will still be worth a kilo of gold.

What this really means to you is the following:

The price of gold remains stable while other currencies fluctuate in relation to it. Over the past 20 years, the price of gold has risen 438.41%, while the dollar has depreciated by the same percentage. Gold is a safe asset for you amid the changing values of debt-based currencies.

WITH GOLD YOU OWN A ZERO-RISK COMMODITY

I recently had a wonderful interview with Andy Schectman of Miles Franklin in the USA, a leading company in the precious metals industry.

My epiphany moment in our interview was when Andy told me that his father had suggested that he start a new business. And the business idea was as simple as a promise. Buy any amount of gold every 14 days. That's a business plan, and it's the exact opposite of buying lottery tickets—which, by the way, is a very bad business plan! So, the only condition was to invest some amount in gold every other week. The deal was, as soon as this was not done, Andy would be out of business. He did it. For about 4 decades now. This business today is a $9 billion company built from the ground up, with no 3rd party investors, or loans, or other outside help!

What if you wanted to put a certain amount of money into gold every other week, and what if there was a plausible solution that would allow you to buy gold—even in smaller amounts—without the huge hassle of transfer management and fees, making it as easy as child's play? Just think about it.

GOLD IS, BY FAR, YOUR BEST DEFENSE AGAINST INFLATION

In short, gold is simply the best way to protect your wealth against inflationary pressures!

Especially in uncertain times, gold gives you security! Gold is the answer to uncertainty. In all global turbulences of the past, people were able to survive the most difficult times and wars without losing everything like millions of others, thanks to gold ownership. So gold shines as a safe haven asset.

THERE ARE TWO DIFFERENT SCENARIOS FOR USING GOLD

In the first scenario, you already have substantial wealth you want to protect. So, gold ownership is about existing wealth and preserving the value of your assets, especially when markets are volatile, as they are today. For you, gold becomes the most comforting refuge when you seek stability in times of uncertainty. Given its strength as a store of value, gold is your shield against market volatility.

We have some world class solutions for you, which we consider to be the safest bank on earth! Feel free to contact us or our team and we will give you the most updated information about your best options.

In the second scenario, you are still in the early stages of building your wealth. In this case, Andy Schectman's father's business idea is exactly what you are looking for. And we can show you how to get the best deals even for smaller amounts. This is not a topic for a book because the adoption rates of technology (Web3, quantum trading, etc.) are so unprecedentedly high that what we would put in this book today would most likely be obsolete before its publication date. Same in this case. We have the right solution at the right time. Just contact us, and our team will be delighted and honored to guide you through!

UNLOCKING FINANCIAL SECURITY: YOUR GOLDEN PATH TO SAFE-GUARDING WEALTH

Today, there are some amazing ways for you to protect your wealth with gold and silver. Historically, gold and silver have been the most reliable medium of exchange and store of wealth. That hasn't changed in thousands of years, and I can't think of a single scenario where that could change in any way in the next 500 years. That's why Reto and I wanted to start with this asset class. But gold in general also helps us explain some of the biggest challenges in the economy today. So, in the next part of this chapter, we also want to focus on the connection between gold and today's challenges. You really want to understand the connection between gold and the bigger picture of cryptocurrencies, tokenization, CBDCs, and so on. And most importantly, you want to see what it means for you to hedge against inflation and fortify your freedom!

Throughout history, gold and silver have played an important role in the creation of currencies. These precious metals have been valued for their scarcity, durability, and intrinsic value. Ancient civilizations such as the Egyptians, Greeks, and Romans recognized the value of these metals and minted coins from them. The use of gold and silver as currency provided a standardized and universally accepted form of payment, facilitating trade and economic transactions. One of the most important advantages of gold and silver as currency is their inherent value. Unlike fiat currencies, or CBDCs (Central Bank Digital Currencies, which the world is moving towards whether we like it or not), which all derive their value from government or central bank decree (and also unlike bitcoin which derives its value from the level of belief in it), gold and silver have intrinsic value due to their scarcity and desirability.

In addition, gold and silver have historically served as a store of value. They have always acted as a hedge against inflation and economic uncertainty.

In times of economic turmoil or currency devaluation, individuals and governments have turned to gold and silver as a safe haven to preserve wealth.

In their great book *Inflation*, Steve Forbes, Elizabeth Ames, and Nathan Lewis write about how to end misery surprisingly quickly, if we understand it properly. I am absolutely agreeing with them that the problem with inflation-fighting approaches—like price controls—is their focus on the symptoms of the problem and not the cause, which is debasing the currency.

Here is what co-author Nathan Lewis calls the Magic Formula:

> *"Stable money and lower taxes. This powerful combination has time and again rescued sliding currencies, and tamed inflation by unleashing vibrant, growing economies with an appetite for money."*

The *Inflation* book also explores the best way to end today's inflation: A return to gold-based money. The authors outline a proposal for a new gold standard that would stabilize the dollar without requiring the country to maintain a gigantic supply of gold:

> *"This system could be implemented in a relatively short time, restoring a sound and stable dollar that would serve as the engine for a new era of entrepreneurial creativity and progress."*

Returning to a gold or silver backed currency will provide a more stable and reliable monetary system. I believe that tying the value of money to gold and silver will limit the ability of governments to manipulate the money supply and thus create excessive inflation. This, in turn, will promote fiscal discipline and protect the purchasing power of individuals.

Of course, this is not what politicians want. Just in 2022, the new US debt reached new records. In just two years, they created twice as much new debt as all the US debt created in the last 200 years.

Let's take a closer look: It took 215 years for the total U.S. debt to reach $7 trillion. From March 2020 to June 2022, they added another $7 trillion. Between June and December 2023, the U.S. debt increased by another $2.6 trillion.

The growth rate of the U.S. national debt is reaching alarming proportions that no one in Washington is even talking about. Now the U.S. national debt is breaking through the astronomical mark of $34 trillion!

As I write this, it has reached a new all-time high of $34,015,705,423,934. Whenever you want, you can watch this live on the Internet by going to:

www.usdebtclock.org

We are in the final editing stage of the book, and the U.S. now has about $225 billion more in total debt, bringing the figure to $34,240,871,610,986—and the clock is ticking. The next screenshot, taken just a few weeks later while this book was in layout, shows an additional increase of over $600 billion. Just imagine— close to one trillion dollars in additional debt incurred during the time it took to write this book.

National debt of the US (June, 2024)

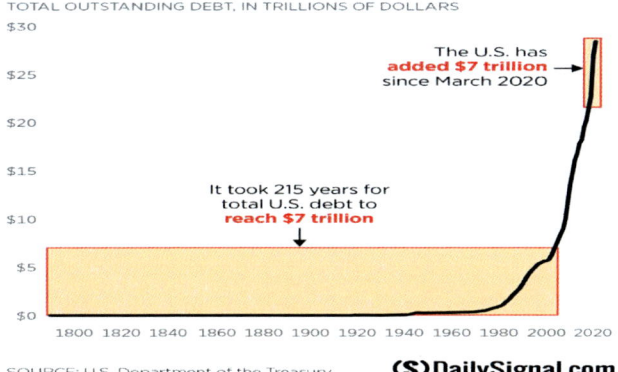

The Staggering Pace of New Debt

TOTAL OUTSTANDING DEBT, IN TRILLIONS OF DOLLARS

The U.S. has **added $7 trillion** since March 2020

It took 215 years for total U.S. debt to **reach $7 trillion**

SOURCE: U.S. Department of the Treasury.

(S) DailySignal.com

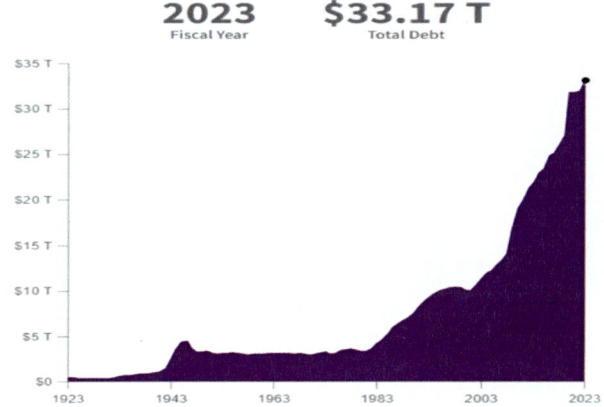

U.S. National Debt Over the Last 100 Years
Inflation Adjusted - 2023 Dollars

2023
Fiscal Year

$33.17 T
Total Debt

Over the past 100 years, the U.S. federal debt has increased from $403 B in 1923 to $33.17 T in 2023.

Visit the Historical Debt Outstanding dataset to explore and download this data. The inflation data is sourced from the Bureau of Labor Statistics. Last Updated: September 30, 2023

Source: https://fiscaldata.treasury.gov/americas-finance-guide/national-debt

https://www.heritage.org/budget-and-spending/commentary/these-7-charts-show-why-congress-must-get-spending-under-control

The amount is so incredible that we have no idea how much $35 trillion really is. I don't think you have an image in your subconscious mind of something worth $35 trillion the way you have an image in your mind of your home, or a Mercedes Benz or any mid-size car, a glass of beer, or your last vacation.

But that is not really the point I want to focus on. I want to make you aware of the following problem that is at the root of all inflation:

GOVERNMENTS NEED NEW MONEY AND **INFLATION IS THE RESULT** BUT THERE IS A WAY OUT!

You have been told all your life that you pay taxes under the illusion that you are funding the government, which you are not!

This is a lie.

Here's the truth in 17 seconds reading time:

Who funds the government? — The government is funded by Treasury bonds. In other words: paper!

Who buys the treasury bonds? — In the US, mostly the FED. In Europe, the ECB.

How do these institutions buy them? — By printing money!

What backing do these institutions have for the money they print? — The treasury bonds themselves!

Do you see? This is the full circle of the fiat brainwashing machine: Money is printed to buy bonds, which then back the newly created money. So, you see, they are basically funding the government by printing money out of thin air!

Now you might ask, "If the government can print unlimited amounts of money out of thin air, why does it collect taxes?" — Now you get it!

. . . .

The real problem is that you are paying high taxes just to maintain the illusion that you are funding the government, which you are not. The government is floating on a sea of paper, creating what's called a "bubble." And bubbles pop!

. . . .

But the situation is worse than it seems, because as more people around the world become aware of this farce, confidence in all currencies will be lost!

Facing this would mean rebuilding our government structure.

Tough choices await...

Such changes can be overwhelming and met with resistance, but know this — your future is yours to shape.

> It will take a total restructuring of government, from top to bottom. It will require hard decisions!

It will be hard. The system will push back, but you have the right to determine your own destiny.

We will come back to this aspect in the chapter "Connection is The New Currency".

So far for now: The solution will be an entirely new category of financial system that promotes trust, independence, efficiency, and inclusiveness.

This system will use gold and silver for its own stability, and it will use the power of "We the People" to create real and lasting freedom. At this point, however, it is very important to recognize that the feasibility and practicality of a gold or silver-based monetary system in the modern world is debatable.

The global economy has become increasingly complex and interconnected, and the transition to such a system could present significant challenges. That's why the ideas I'm about to present to you are designed to provide three essential features:

1) 100% Privacy
2) 100% Trust
3) 100% Efficiency

Let me add a very rare peculiarity to the background of what I'm talking about.

Surprisingly, my introduction to gold came through the extraordinary book *Unfair Crypto Advantage* by Jens Krautscheid, and a period in my business life when I was asked to join the board of a Swiss AG, a global company specializing in gold tokenization. I served this company as their Global Director of Strategic Partnerships and learned a lot about gold and crypto. I want to share some of my biggest "Aha Moments" with you because I know that these truths are not really known by many people.

First of all, during my time with this Swiss company that promotes digital gold and silver, I used to ask myself, "Why would I want digital gold when I can have real gold?" The same goes for silver. Of course, we can argue that the fractalization that comes with digital tokens is a wonderful thing—and yes, it definitely is—and I think that is where the future lies - but only part of the future.

There are a lot of good people working on that future behind the scenes. But right now, I can't recommend any of the digital gold players out there. There are some good ideas out there, but not yet in a state where we can really rely on them. Anyway, let us see what we have for sure.

Reto, did you know that cryptocurrencies are not Sharia-compliant? Yes, Gisi, I know that. I'm involved in various blockchain-based projects, and I do business with Dubai-based companies, and I heard that there are religious factors that don't allow Muslims to invest in crypto. But to be honest, this is not my biggest strength.

Well, it is good that I brought up this very important aspect. We all need to know that Middle Eastern countries with large Muslim populations are increasingly developing regulatory frameworks for cryptocurrencies. And since we are living in a time of huge global changes, I really believe that we would all do well to understand the consequences of cryptocurrencies (as a matter of fact, most of them—including bitcoin and ETH—are not compliant with Sharia rules) and what it means for us to invest in a system that is fully compliant with these rules.

For me—and believe me, I still think of myself as a crypto baby just out of diapers—there are basically two types of cryptocurrencies: The first one has a volatility problem. Price fluctuations are risky and unpredictable, which makes them very interesting for risk-taking investors. This is because there are incredible profits to be made. As long as things go well and you don't have a problem losing your money, it's certainly a very exciting thing. The second type: Stable coins! They are stable but do not offer exceptional prospects because they are systematically pegged to another stable value (like the USDC to the Dollar). Here's the thing: both types of cryptocurrencies have one thing in common! Many people do not know how they work. They are too complicated and therefore not yet widely accepted. Their usefulness as a real alternative to traditional money is limited. Because of regulatory uncertainties and other concerns, most people continue to use worthless paper money ("in God we trust") and banks. This is true for all cryptos today, in short: people don't understand them because either one is just too cryptic!

Now allow me to get a little further away from our original topic, which of course is not crypto, but gold and money for freedom. But I want you to get the bigger picture.

Do you know Apple's first print ad? I have it for you... —flip the page and enjoy:

Apple Introduces the First Low Cost Microcomputer System with a Video Terminal and 8K Bytes of RAM on a Single PC Card.

The Apple Computer. A truly complete microcomputer system on a single PC board. Based on the MOS Technology 6502 microprocessor, the Apple also has a built-in video terminal and sockets for 8K bytes of on-board RAM memory. With the addition of a keyboard and video monitor, you'll have an extremely powerful computer system that can be used for anything from developing programs to playing games or running BASIC.

Combining the computer, video terminal and dynamic memory on a single board has resulted in a large reduction in chip count, which means more reliability and lowered cost. Since the Apple comes fully assembled, tested & burned-in and has a complete power supply on-board, initial set-up is essentially "hassle free" and you can be running within minutes. At $666.66 (including 4K bytes RAM!) it opens many new possibilities for users and systems manufacturers.

You Don't Need
an Expensive Teletype.

Using the built-in video terminal and keyboard interface, you avoid all the expense, noise and maintenance associated with a teletype. And the Apple video terminal is six times faster than a teletype, which means more throughput and less waiting. The Apple connects directly to a video monitor (or home TV with an inexpensive RF modulator) and displays 960 easy to read characters in 24 rows of 40 characters per line with automatic scrolling. The video display section contains its own 1K bytes of memory, so all the RAM memory is available for user programs. And the

Keyboard Interface lets you use almost any ASCII-encoded keyboard.

The Apple Computer makes it possible for many people with limited budgets to step up to a video terminal as an I/O device for their computer.

No More Switches,
No More Lights.

Compared to switches and LED's, a video terminal can display vast amounts of information simultaneously. The Apple video terminal can display the contents of 192 memory locations at once on the screen. And the firmware in PROMS enables you to enter, display and debug programs (all in hex) from the keyboard, rendering a front panel unnecessary. The firmware also allows your programs to print characters on the display, and since you'll be looking at letters and numbers instead of just LED's, the door is open to all kinds of alphanumeric software (i.e., Games and BASIC).

8K Bytes RAM in 16 Chips!

The Apple Computer uses the new 16-pin 4K dynamic memory chips. They are faster and take ¾ the space and power of even the low power 2102's (the memory chip that everyone else uses). That means 8K bytes in sixteen chips. It also means no more 28 amp power supplies.

The system is fully expandable to 65K via an edge connector which carries both the address and data busses, power supplies and all timing signals. All dynamic memory refreshing for both on and off-board memory is done automatically. Also, the Apple Computer can be upgraded to use the 16K chips when they become availa-

ble. That's 32K bytes on-board RAM in 16 IC's—the equivalent of 256 2102's!

A Little Cassette Board
That Works!

Unlike many other cassette boards on the marketplace, ours works every time. It plugs directly into the upright connector on the main board and stands only 2" tall. And since it is very fast (1500 bits per second), you can read or write 4K bytes in about 20 seconds. All timing is done in software, which results in crystal-controlled accuracy and uniformity from unit to unit.

Unlike some other cassette interfaces which require an expensive tape recorder, the Apple Cassette Interface works reliably with almost any audio-grade cassette recorder.

Software:

A tape of **APPLE BASIC** is included free with the Cassette Interface. Apple Basic features immediate error messages and fast execution, and lets you program in a higher level language immediately and without added cost. Also available **now** are a dis-assembler and many games, with many software packages, (including a macro assembler) in the works. And since our philosophy is to provide software for our machines free or at minimal cost, you won't be continually paying for access to this growing software library.

The Apple Computer is in stock at almost all major computer stores. (If your local computer store doesn't carry our products, encourage them or write us direct). **Dealer inquiries invited.**

Byte into an Apple $666.66*
* includes 4K bytes RAM

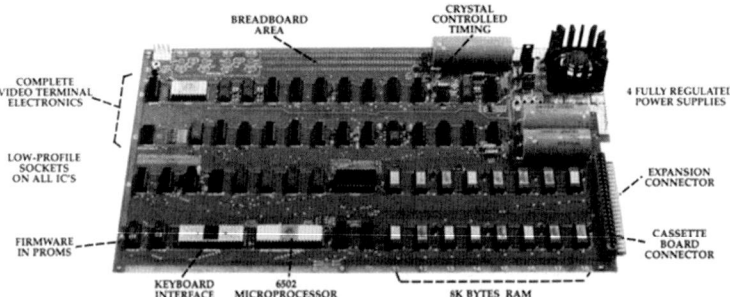

COMPLETE VIDEO TERMINAL ELECTRONICS

LOW-PROFILE SOCKETS ON ALL IC'S

FIRMWARE IN PROMS

KEYBOARD INTERFACE

6502 MICROPROCESSOR

8K BYTES RAM

BREADBOARD AREA

CRYSTAL CONTROLLED TIMING

4 FULLY REGULATED POWER SUPPLIES

EXPANSION CONNECTOR

CASSETTE BOARD CONNECTOR

APPLE Computer Company • 770 Welch Rd., Palo Alto, CA 94304 • (415) 326-4248

OCTOBER 1976   CIRCLE NO. 7 ON INQUIRY CARD   INTERFACE AGE 11

Do you want some Low-Profile Sockets On All IC's?

Let me just point out a few of the highlights for you:

The Apple Computer uses the new 16-pin, 4K, dynamic **memory chips. They are faster and take ¼ the space and power of** even the low power 2102's *(the memory chip that everyone else uses).* That means 8K bytes in sixteen chips. *It also means no more* 28-amp power supplies. *The system is* fully expandable to 65K via an edge connector *which carries both the address and data busses.*

Isn't this absolutely amazing?

I bet you wake up in the mornings, and even before you jump out of the bed, you think: 'today I need to get a **firmware in PROMS** that enables me to enter, display, and debug programs. **And the best part is, it's all in hex!**'

All in hex! This is how crypto looks to the world today.

What if we can make it simple?

WHAT IF WE CAN
MAKE IT
GOLDEN?

How did Apple go from that first cryptic ad to one of the biggest companies in the world, with arguably some of the best marketing you'll find? They simplified everything—KISS—keep it simple, stupid!

What about the following?

Connection Is The New Currency

Your Payments Made Easy

Money For Freedom!

Powered by **BE!** Better Earth

Well, so much for the world of advertising: I wanted to make a point.

Crypto's problem is the same problem Apple created with its 1976 ad. The problem is one word:

Complexity!

As a result, only one in a million people truly understand the inherent nuances of both the digital and traditional money systems and the profound impact that they have on your life.

Financial literacy isn't taught in school, so many people are unaware of its underlying intricacies. Our goal is to demystify the complexities for you and bring clarity to your financial understanding.

WHAT BRINGS ME BACK TO YOU

If you are a gambler, crypto is a wild market to gamble your investments. I wish you good luck! I also gamble; wish me luck, too. But when it comes to a serious alternative payment system that works globally and is trustworthy, I simply believe there should be no roulette aspects involved. What do you think? I just wish for something that makes, say, fiat obsolete and the old crypto look like a Palm Pilot compared to the iPhone; we come back to that idea…

And believe it or not, there is a solution! What I call Money for Freedom is designed to give you the ability to unbank yourself and put your wealth into a secure system that is not influenced by governments or central banks. Imagine a sound monetary system that offers gold and silver at your fingertips for instant payments anywhere in the world: Hundreds of millions, even billions of people without bank accounts, equipped instead with cell phones, could benefit from access to fractionalized gold and silver.

....

This is what I want Money for Freedom to be:

1) Freedom from Government Influence: Achieve financial independence by avoiding government interference.

2) Freedom from Restrictions: Enjoy fast, low-cost transactions worldwide, with the option of using an unlimited card.

....

Freedom from locations that can be compromised or seized. With Money for Freedom's decentralized finance, you say goodbye to middlemen like banks; you have more control and flexibility in managing your funds.

Now: Imagine a Swiss company extending this benefit globally, reaching people in Venezuela or Buenos Aires, in African villages, in Lebanon and beyond. On the other hand, individuals like you with bank accounts can unbank, exit fiat, and find peace of mind in the value of your money with a safe store against inflation.

And now we come full circle in this very intense chapter: 100% Sharia-compliant: Money for Freedom is based on 100% asset-backed transactions that are fully Sharia-compliant. Trust and ethics come first: Being Sharia-compliant isn't just about following religious laws.

It means conducting business in an ethical and responsible manner, which is essential for all human beings. This system is being built as we write and is positioned to be the counterpart to the complexities of the financial system, banks, SWIFT, CBDCs, and today's crypto valleys.

WHAT BRINGS US BACK TO GOLD

Gold is simply the most enduring store of value in all of history.

Gold is simply the most sought-after precious metal in the world.

Gold is also the most reliable hedge against economic uncertainty.

Gold is simply the most universally recognized symbol of wealth and prosperity.

Gold is the most resilient asset in times of market volatility.

Gold is simply the most trusted form of currency in times of crisis.

Gold is simply the most timeless and elegant form of jewelry.

Gold is simply the most coveted prize in prestigious awards and competitions.

Gold is simply the most enduring testament to human craftsmanship and artistry.

And gold is simply the most enduring symbol of love and commitment, as seen in wedding rings around the world.

I hope I didn't use the word "simply" too much. Of course, I used it on purpose, because instead of more complexity, we need more simplicity for solutions that really change the world.

And we need change while change is possible. CBDCs (Central Banks Digital Currencies) are just around the corner. Many of my best contacts—highly placed and highly informed—are making the point that the battle is already lost. I don't (want to) give in on this point.

YOU NEED A SIMPLE SOLUTION

Some people are aware of CBDCs and have taken steps to prepare, while others are either unaware of the potential effects of digital control and dictatorship or are choosing to wait and see how things develop before taking action.

Many cling to what's familiar and are wary of change. The concept of a CBDC can seem complex, but it's designed to simplify financial processes, not complicate them. While cryptocurrencies may be confusing to you, a CBDC promises a seamless transition to a more straightforward system. But it is a trap!

You run on programs in every area of your life, and when it comes to banking and money for freedom, it needs to rewrite a program that is deeply installed: Opening a local bank account is usually a simple and straightforward process, while setting up a cryptocurrency account can be unfamiliar and somewhat daunting for some.

The very nature of the newness of cryptocurrencies ("all in hex"), as opposed to the physical presence of traditional banks, can make them seem intangible and more difficult to trust.

Here's the trap: those in power pushing central bank digital currencies (CBDCs) seem to be taking small steps-each one incrementally limiting our freedoms.

Think of slowly boiling frogs: The slow erosion of freedoms often goes unnoticed until significant change is forced upon us. Many out there have become complacent, unwilling to venture into change unless it promises a definite positive outcome. Unfortunately, sometimes the realization of the need for change comes too late—when the metaphorical roof is already in flames. I have worked with more than 12,000 people, one-on-one, in seminars, off- and online, and most people share the same pattern. They put off change until the very last moment. Change can be easy and fun when it is early and not necessary at all. The motivation is mere curiosity, adventurousness, and love for the new. If you do that, the whole process of change can be so enjoyable. But change is hard and can be very painful when it is desperately needed because your house is on fire. Do you understand what I mean? If the masses accept the CBDCs because they are pushing them everywhere and the process will be easy, you are in a trap! Then it's too late!

DON'T WAIT!
WAITING IS A TRAP!

Reto and I can provide you with a Swiss bank account with total privacy, inflation proof currencies, global payments, unlimited cards, risk free 7% returns, and tax-free capital gains.

And because the ecosystem is based on 100% asset-backed transactions, and trust and ethics are paramount, the system is 100% Sharia-compliant. It's not just about following religious laws. It is about conducting business in an ethical and responsible manner, which is essential for all human beings.

Basically, the whole idea is based on civil rights, which I think makes it unstoppable because it positions itself as the antithesis of the controversial banking practices of the last century. The company's mission is to restore integrity, trust, and privacy to banking by offering customers a safe, transparent, and ethical alternative.

There are other systems in the works as we write this book, and I bet by the time you read it there will be tons of news and proven facts that we will want to share with you. It will be our honor and pleasure to do so. Connect!

Amazing, Gisi! And again, we, the Swiss, did not invent the banking system. We did not reinvent it or improve it fundamentally. We simply added one very important factor. Trust! And now anyone can use and benefit from this Swiss trust factor without having to travel to this tiny little country in the Alps. Anyone can use it anywhere in the world.

So, like you, Gisi, I'm betting on the great future of gold!

....

If you, dear reader, believe that too, and you'd like some more guidance on how you can benefit from some amazing systems, just contact me and I'll be happy to give you more details; you can email my office. I'll answer them all - just give me a little of your patience. You can reach my office at support@wgw-advisors.com

....

P.S.: It may take up to a week to get my answer, but I promise I will answer you.

LET'S GET PHYSICAL WITH
GOLD AND SILVER AT HOME

Speed Read: You should have working solutions for crazy situations like hyperinflation or Internet blackouts. Physical coins in the form of silver ounces and gold ounces at home. Keep precious metals on hand as purchasing power for those times we all hope never to experience. Aside from being the solution to extreme circumstances, it feels great to have them in your hands—every day!

We are still in our cash reserves section. We were talking about the "two types" of cryptocurrencies that you mentioned, Gisi. Certainly, digital currencies are one of the forward-looking trends that are taking off, and we will come to BTC next. If you also see what's happening in the direction of digital francs, digital euros, digital US dollars, and so on, it's certainly one of the strongest trends that physical money is going to disappear. On the other hand, there is another aspect of using gold and silver that has stood the test of time, as mentioned in the previous chapter, for thousands of years. And that aspect is that I believe you should have physical coins in your home in the form of ounces of silver and ounces of gold. And—believe it or not—the solution we just talked about also brings your gold into your home. Ask me if you want to know more.

Yes, thank you for mentioning that, Reto. If you are like me, you also like to touch things that are valuable to you! There was a time in my life when I always carried at least one, but usually several 500 Euro bills in my wallet. Not because I needed to have 2,000 or 3,000 Euros with me; I just love the feeling and the energy of having them with me. You know I teach a lot about e-motion, energy in motion, which is the cause of everything we are, do, and have in our lives. So, when I am in any place paying for any goods or services and I take out a 50 Euro bill or maybe just a 10 or 20 Euro bill, I consciously touch and feel the 500 Euro bills and that brings me back to these 5 steps. 1) Feeling love and gratitude, 2) Believing that where those $500 bills came from, there will be much more for my family and for me and for all these great personalities that I do business with, and on that e-motion I can easily continue to 3) Be, 4) Do and 5) Have what I love to be, do, and have.

What I mean is that it is impossible to create that feeling with an icon and a few pixels on your phone while paying with your wallet. Especially when it comes to high value items, the haptic is indispensable for me. It is the same with holding and opening a great book or reading it on any reader. I love both, but there is no substitute for touching, opening, and even smelling a book. These feelings are powerful! Do you remember Vinyl Disks and how it was when you got the latest one from one of your music idols? It got lost with the CD (just because it was not the same feeling as opening the big album cover and holding it in your hand). But today on Spotify or Deezer, it's just a memory. So, I am a haptic fan. It is wonderful to have some fractionalized gold and silver at the tip of my finger on my iPhone, but I think there is nothing like having a real gold or silver coin in your hand. Sitting at home and holding your gold in your hand creates an e-motion of abundance, and that is the only frequency at which we can really become successful investors.

Yes, I agree, that feeling is something that digital assets simply cannot give us. But there is much more to it: if you have gold and silver with you, you have a constant value with you. What do we do with crypto if the Internet goes down? Or what if the CBDCs (Central Bank Digital Currencies) are installed and they don't like what you sent on WhatsApp or Signal, and they decide to confiscate your digital cash? Did you know that in China, if you run a red light, the fine is immediately deducted from your digital account? What if you don't comply with the latest health measures and you can't access your digital coins because of your individual point of view? In the past decades, we have seen several cases where countries ran out of cash in ATMs—see Iceland or Greece. That's why I think it's a must for every investor and sound money advocate to have a portion of your wealth in physical gold and silver at home. Sure, Gisi, the haptic is great and also the feeling of having these values at hand, but I just want to focus more on the benefits you have when you own some physical coins as silver ounces and gold ounces.

The price of gold changes. But if you adjust it for inflation, you get the same amount for an ounce of gold today as you did for an ounce of gold many years ago. In other words, it has really held its value for centuries or even millennia, which is why I think it makes perfect sense to always have some gold and silver coins at home for emergencies, for your cash reserve.

A silver coin is about 30 Swiss francs right now, and I can do a good week's shopping with that if things get critical, or if we have hyperinflation, if we somehow can't get money from the bank - whatever may come. If I have silver coins, I'm safe because I can make my purchases because silver has held its value over the last few centuries. Gold coins certainly make sense because they just have a much higher value. I cannot make my daily household purchases, but perhaps can make larger purchases with a gold coin.

In 1971, President Nixon went off the gold standard, and the way the price of gold has gone since then is pretty amazing. Back then, an ounce of gold—about 30 grams—was about 35 dollars. Today, the ounce is around 2,100 dollars. So that is also a safe value; if you have it at home, it has increased 60 times in 60 years. A 6,000 percent increase in value! That's what I call *The Swiss Wealth Creation.*

It doesn't look quite as extreme with silver, but again, it was $1.30 then and it's $24 now - the same coin. Both precious metals belong in my portfolio. But I keep them at home, and I can only recommend that you do the same.

. . . .

If you want to get firsthand advice, don't hesitate to send an email to my office—I will definitely be happy to give you some valuable tips: support@wgw-advisors.com.

. . . .

BITCOIN IS THE
STRONGEST DIGITAL CURRENCY

Speed Read: Bitcoin: The strongest digital currency needs to be in your portfolio—this chapter could end here. I don't think I can tell you anything new that you can't find on every corner of the Internet ;-)

We spent a long time discussing gold and its connections to the financial world, including CBDCs and cryptocurrencies. Don't get us wrong; we are not "against" crypto. We are just looking over the horizon, and at least I feel that the current crypto world is like the smart phones of 2004 or 2006. Do you remember them? The ones like the "Nokia Communicator" or the "BlackBerry" with keyboard and "Internet"; but as Steve Jobs rightly said when he introduced the first iPhone to the world: All those other smartphones were "not so smart" at all! In fact, they had "baby Internet" compared to Apple, and many other shortcomings. So, when I look beyond crypto, I see a completely different scene than today. With solutions that make the current crypto scene look like BlackBerries and Nokias. That said, I not only believe that some of these old crypto dinosaurs will survive, I also believe you will be best off having some of them in your pocket. Or rather, your wallet!

Reto, over to you, please guide us through your priceless knowledge about Bitcoin.

Yes, Gisi, I'm glad to share more. We are still talking about ways to build your reserves. It could be a precious metals savings plan, a strategic metals savings plan, or a bitcoin savings plan. "Hm, a BTC savings plan? Why would I need that? Can't I just go on the Internet and buy some bitcoins?"—You can, but a bitcoin savings plan allows you to smooth out the high volatility of the cryptocurrency over time. In other words, you buy cheaper one day and maybe more expensive the next, but you have an average cost effect in the long run. With the average cost advantage, you can build another financial pillar that I think belongs in every portfolio. You do not have to risk too much of your money; use BTC to a small extent so that you can participate, because I also see bitcoin as a huge opportunity in the future. I think it is another important neutral currency in the market. I don't know where it's going to go, but I'm convinced that if you put money into it on a regular basis over the next 15 years, you're going to have a very, very large fortune on the side that you might be able to reallocate to other assets at some point.

Interesting! Is there a specific reason why you say 15 years from now, Reto? I generally know people who advise others to put a certain amount into BTC today, like "take 20% of your savings and put it into Bitcoin and Ethereum and just wait", and this approach of a long-term savings plan is really something completely different.

I always think very long-term, Gisi - ideally, ten years for many investments. It's interesting that investors often say ten years, but subconsciously they mean two to three years, so I prefer a slightly longer horizon of ten to 15 years, and if, after five to ten years, we have a great success, even better. But with the long-term horizon, we certainly have the very, very good results that we want to achieve.

DUTY-FREE STORAGE
OF PRECIOUS METALS

Speed read: Why a bonded warehouse?

You don't pay VAT, you don't have too large a quantity at home, everything is fully insured, and the customs themselves will take care of and protect your assets!

Preserving value is a topic that always concerns me, and I think it should concern you because I keep seeing hard-working people who are actually destroying their money because they take it to the bank. And then inflation eats up the value. There are simply better options.

We've talked about having gold and silver coins at home as an emergency reserve. That's one option, which of course has to do with preserving value, even in crisis, in addition to building up your reserves. The other option is to keep a little more than just a nest egg in gold and silver or other precious metals in a bonded warehouse. Why in a bonded warehouse? There are several reasons for this. Gold is considered a currency; all other precious metals are tangible assets and are subject to VAT. So, if I buy silver or platinum and palladium and store them in a bonded warehouse, I don't pay VAT. In Switzerland, it is 8.1 percent; in Germany, it is 19 percent. That means you get 8.1 or 19 percent more goods in your bonded warehouse than if you make the same investment at a bank or a precious metal dealer and take the physical precious metal home with you. And you can purchase the precious metals at wholesale prices, even small quantities, while they charge you up to 20%, sometimes even more, for small quantities at the precious metal dealer.

So that's a huge advantage that bonded warehouses offer. Another advantage that I also see is that you don't have too large a quantity at home. You might have a queasy feeling in your stomach. And that doesn't happen if you have your valuables in a well-supplied bonded warehouse where everything is fully insured. Care is taken to ensure that everything is handled 100 percent in accordance with the law and you have nothing to do with it. So, it's well insured in Switzerland and also protected from government access, and independent from your bank. It really is a great way to protect a portion of your assets in this way, and this portion will of course also increase in value, i.e., you will benefit from the preservation of value for many, many years. In case you need liquidation, you will get it in a very short time since physical silver and gold is easy to sell.

Reto, the nice thing is that you have your property in a very safe place and the customs themselves also take care of your property. The distinction that it's *your* property is important, dear reader, because when you give your money to the bank, it is no longer your money, it is the property of the bank, and you are only a creditor.

What's in the bonded warehouse is 100% your property and customs. Believe me, they do a good job. They take care of your property because they want it to stay there! Otherwise, somebody would have to pay 19 or 8.1% tax on it, so protecting it so that it does not leave the vault is their job. That's another background that I find very exciting - that the customs officers of your country are also taking care of your property. A nice side effect!

And in Switzerland, and Liechtenstein in particular, many companies have specialized in building these high-security warehouses to store these assets and take advantage of these many benefits.

How to double your gold assets: I love this strategy! By knowing the gold—silver ratio, you can double your gold assets in the long term. When the ratio is over 1:80, I prefer to buy silver. When you know that less silver is mined each year than is used in the industry, you know it is undervalued. Also, the gold to silver production ratio is 1:7, which also shows that silver is undervalued. And when you know that there are 429 times more paper exchanges than physical silver (every ounce of physical silver is sold 429 times around the world!), you know that there will be a war when everyone wants their silver assets in physical form.

People often tell me that gold and silver pay no interest. I say: Thank God! If it paid interest, I would have to pay income tax on it. If it is just a capital gain, there is usually no income tax on it. (Check with your tax advisor; each country may be different).

If you have a business and cash available within your business, you can even use a business owner strategy to build your personal wealth tax free and grow your retirement plan. I will be happy to discuss this option with you.

Once again, the more financially literate you are, the better financial decisions you can make.

Did you know that there are 2 different types of bonded warehouses? Open Customs Warehouses (OCW) and Duty-Free Warehouses (DFW). The Open Customs Warehouses (OCW) are, by law, a tax-free customs area. For these warehouses, the Swiss customs authorities have access to the stock accounts in order to carry out periodic audits. Your goods will be supervised by a private OCW operator who will post a bond with the customs authorities to ensure the correct handling of the goods. Depending on the operator, you may have 24/7 access to your assets, which is important when dramatic scenarios occur, such as the enforcement of new laws, which often happen over a weekend.

To gain access to Duty-Free Warehouses (DFW), you must pass through Swiss Customs, which operates from 8-5, Monday through Friday.

So, OCW can be an advantage for your precious metals, while the DFW is fine for limited art. With access to precious metals over the weekend or holidays, you are very flexible to react in stressful situations; with art, you can usually wait until the next business day.

Again, with the right financial education, you can be even more prepared for any crisis.

THE POWER OF
STRATEGIC METALS

Speed read: Industrial metals give you flexibility.

This is a very unknown investment class! It is precisely because these are so unknown that Industrial metals or strategic metals —two terms that mean the same— are so unknown that enormous profits are possible.

With precious metals, it is very important to have flexibility. This means that once I have the need, I can bring the metals back onto the market promptly, and with gold and silver, platinum, and palladium, this is easy because the demand is there on the market.

A very good alternative to precious metals is strategic metals, an area that is very unknown, but there are also opportunities to store these strategic metals that are used in industry in a bonded warehouse, with the same benefits that we have seen with precious metals.

It is very important that we work with a supplier that has very good relationships in the industry. That means that when you want to sell these strategic metals, these industrial metals like gallium, hafnium and indium, germanium, rhenium, terbium oxide and dysprosium oxide can be sold.

Often, we are not even aware of all the industrial metals that are used, whether it is in a cell phone, an X-ray machine, or the entire automotive or solar industry. So many different metals are used, and there is a huge demand in the future! It is going to increase, and we are going to see all the prices climb even higher. So, I see this as a wonderful addition to the portfolio - to be able to acquire a number of different industrial metals, have them in the duty-free warehouse, and then be able to sell them as needed or have them in the bonded warehouse for a longer period of time as another asset. In 2022, hafnium alone tripled its value. Nevertheless, again, it is important to have diversification and have all strategic metals in your portfolio so that market price changes even out your ROI.

DISCOVERING
LIMITED ART

Speed read: This is not about Mona Lisa or Van Goghs. It is about a highly predictable investment opportunity that makes it possible for the "small investor" to invest like the largest global hedge funds or major banks and security companies.

In this chapter, I would like to introduce you to another opportunity that few people know about, but which is also related to the big topic of tax-free warehouses: Investing in art.

If you're like most people, Mona Lisa comes to mind, or some Rembrandt or other world-famous living artist like Gerhard Richter - artists who have created unique pieces that are sometimes worth millions. That's a very interesting topic, but that's not the point here.

I had the same experience as you. At first, I also thought of the Van Goghs and Dalis of this world, but I was able to learn from a very special connoisseur. It's true that buying such a rare work of art is or can be a great investment, but purchases of unique pieces are always individual deals between sellers and buyers. The deal is as unique as the painting itself. This means that there is no real market value for your investment. A unique work of art has no market volume. There are only individual collectors.

On top — did you know that about 95% of all Rembrandt paintings are copies, not originals? The reason is that Rembrandt let all his students paint his originals so that no one could see a difference.

Now, for your *Swiss Wealth Creation*, you want a portfolio that is also very predictable! You want market volume and a market price. Without it, it will sometimes be very difficult to impossible to sell if you decide to liquidate in the future, which is why I'm so glad I discovered this opportunity I'm about to tell you about:

Limited Edition Contemporary Photography! What is this? Photographs by renowned artists known on at least three continents and exhibited in the largest galleries and museums in the world. Be it the Museum of Modern Art or Art Basel. These are artists who have a big name and reputation. They often do photo series of ten to twenty prints, so the number is limited, and these photographic artworks are very elaborate, so you have a limited series that you can use for your personal wealth protection.

With a limited series, you can find out the different prices that have already been paid for the individual pictures on the market. You can go back to the existing market and get an average price, so you know what these works of art are worth on the open market and the whole thing is very easy to calculate. That also makes it easier for the insurance companies because they get all the prices, they have a central database, and they make a confirmation of the Insurance Value every year. So, you always know what your art is worth.

These limited-edition photographs are also stored in bonded warehouses, and they are always exhibited in the major galleries and museums, especially with emerging artists, The more famous an artist becomes, the more they are exhibited in major galleries, the more they get to be known, and the more valuable your limited-edition artwork of that artist becomes.

It is very important that the piece of art is registered in your name. This means that you have the warehouse receipt at home. The art is yours and you can access it at any time. If you wish, you can take the pieces out of the bonded warehouse and hang them in your home. Then you must pay the VAT, but you have some beautiful pictures on the wall. Then you have another value that really makes you independent because the asset itself is independent. Independent of the stock market, independent of other asset classes, independent of the economy, precious metal prices, weather conditions, strikes, …independent of your bank… independent of…

… exactly: Inflation! — These limited editions make you independent of inflation because the intrinsic value they contain is simply not subject to the market fluctuations associated with fiat money. Precious metals, strategic metals, and limited-edition art are therefore like a rock in the surf when it comes to navigating values safely and independently through stormy times with high inflation rates and an average value growth of over 10% every year.

Above all, this store of value solution is something that large, globally positioned hedge funds, and the largest banks and insurance companies, continue to buy. I have been told that Die Deutsche Bank has 10 to 15 percent of its assets invested in art (for more than 55,000 pieces of art!), and I think you will agree, that the following is one of the most important points: If the big banks can do this, then we as comparatively small investors—at least compared to a big bank, insurance company, or global hedge fund—should look for ways to do the same.

The opportunity I have found—and I am very proud and happy about it—makes it possible to offer this phenomenal *Swiss Wealth Creation* instrument to the "normal" investor. Thanks to this opportunity that I can offer, it is really possible for the "small investor" to follow what is possible for huge institutional investors, and to use the same mechanisms as the "big players"! And it becomes easy for you to further diversify your portfolio in a very lucrative way and profit from this very special market. This gives you independence, and that is what I want for you.

EXCLUSIVE INSIGHTS INTO
DIAMONDS

Speed read: The world's smallest asset for its value. Stored at home or in duty-free storage.

Easy to take with you.

Certified by institutions like GIA, they have a fixed value all over the globe.

If we look at the very wealthy, they very often have diamonds in every portfolio. Diamonds also have a particularly high value, so they are certainly not an option for every portfolio, but I was amazed at the price at which I can include one-carat diamonds in my portfolio.

What is so special about diamonds? From my point of view, there are a few things that stand out: Firstly, it's the smallest store of value in the world. I can pack so much value into a few grams, it's incredible. You can put billions in just a handful of these little wonderful stones. Diamonds also became very well-known thanks to the Jews, who were very often expelled, and so they could easily pack their valuables into small bags and take them with them. So, diamonds have a very high value in a very small space, and they can be transported very easily over long distances, which is more difficult with a single-family home, or even with gold or silver. Not to mention carrying around a Rembrandt or a Monet and damaging a corner of the artwork on the baggage carousel at the airport. Just kidding, but you get my point. With diamonds, you can literally put a few billion dollars of wealth in your pocket!

All the aristocratic houses, without exception, have diamonds in their safes as a store of value because diamonds have simply always retained their value over time.

Diamonds have a very high level of acceptance in the world. It is also very important that the diamonds that you take into a portfolio as an investor are also certified by one of the largest certification bodies in the world, the GIA, so that you can take the diamond to a dealer at any time, anywhere in the world. The dealer can then read the reference number from the diamond, which is lasered into it in very small letters, and he knows exactly what he is holding in his hands because it is certified.

Diamonds are a perfect store of value, whether at home or in a bonded warehouse. With our provider, less than 1% of all cut diamonds meet the criteria of investment diamonds, and that is the niche you need to focus on. Diamonds are an investor's best friend!

We have now covered two of the three most important building blocks of *The Swiss Wealth Creation*—cash reserves and asset protection. We now come to the third important module - asset accumulation.

A great area for asset accumulation is start-ups. This is a topic that is becoming more and more important and increasingly interesting for non-institutional investors because, thanks to the Internet and Web3, it is becoming easier and easier for you and me to participate.

I like to say that I love it when people have more problems, because then more problem solvers and solutions are needed, and you often get them through start-ups.

START-UP
BUSINESSES

Speed read: You invest directly into new businesses in early or late stages.

Know their business model, know their team, know their added value!

Investing in a startup is a completely different topic because there are different stages and phases in a startup. It can be in the early startup, but it can also be in later stages, which means it is already very advanced. You certainly have the greatest potential to increase your money a lot in the early startups, but if you invest in a company very, very early, of course, the risk is often very high because most of them fail. This, in turn, explains and justifies the large profits in the cases when they turn into very big successes.

Anyone who can imagine having invested in Facebook very, very early on knows that it can really pay off in the long run. But it is always difficult to pick the companies and put them in the right context. One could also have invested in Friendster in 2002.

Friendster was by far the biggest network at this time, see https://en.wikipedia.org/wiki/Friendster, but it shut down in 2015, so that investment would have been gone. It also makes sense to build a broader portfolio within the startup asset class. We will come back to this later in the book when we talk about investment clubs. One strategy can be to invest in different startups with the investment club in order to simply spread the risk even more.

A very important point with startups is: What kind of management is behind it? Who runs the company? Is the person running the company alone or is there a whole team behind it? Has the management team successfully launched other projects? What is the company's liquidity? What is the business plan? Is it a realistic scenario or a dreamer's dream based on hopes and fantasies? When you talk to the CEO or the founders, how do they come across? Do they know exactly what they are doing? Or is there a lot of uncertainty? Are they teachable or do they already know everything better?

These are all points that I have to weigh for myself to decide whether I want to invest or not. Another very interesting point with startups is a question you can ask yourself: Do you want to be actively involved, or do you want to be a passive investor?

As a passive investor, you just give them the money and let them work. With an active investment, you can imagine joining the board of directors or the advisory board to help make certain decisions. These are also points that you can control in the startup.

The entire value chain of the startup is certainly the most important of all. Is it the product or service the market is looking for? How will the income be made? For me, this is the key question for any business: how does a company earn money?

For the inexperienced investor, it can then be an alternative to expect slightly lower returns, but to invest in a company that is already further along has already made its first sales, has already received its first feedback from the market, and is already involved in large-scale production, enables you to see that the company has very good standing and potential for the future. In this stadium, the companies have already raised the share price, so you won't have the same yield, but you will have much more security.

The profile of the investor is very, very important. Ask yourself:

— "What can I invest in, and what do I want to invest in?"

— "Where am I willing to go, and how deep do I want to go into the individual startups?"

There are also very, very good opportunities in later stages. They usually do this to take another step, to scale the production, and to expand into other countries. These are always big steps that require a lot of money, and then they go out and do another round of financing. This can be very exciting for us as investors - to get in and benefit from the higher share prices, either as capital gains or, later, as we get cash flow from dividends.

CONVERTIBLE
LOANS

Speed read: With a convertible loan, you get the opportunity to provide financing to a company — also investing in established businesses — while having the potential to convert the loan into equity in the future. It offers flexibility and potential upside.

A very exciting opportunity is also to invest in established companies that have the next big step ahead of them, be it an IPO or a sale of the company. What often happens when a company is to be sold is that the intrinsic value must be as high as possible. The higher the enterprise value, the higher the selling price. Companies then consider how they can increase this intrinsic value. One of these possibilities is that if they have more money, they can then place larger orders, and that increased liquidity can also bring more value to the company.

Companies may then look for loans to do this, which brings us to one of the most exciting options for me: convertible loans.

This means that you give the company a loan, and at a later date, you have the option of either getting your loan and the interest back or converting your loan into shares. This gives you the opportunity to see how the company has developed over time, and only then do you decide whether you want to continue investing in the company, whether you want shares in the company, or whether you say, "No, I just want the interest and my money back" - and you have both options.

So, convertible bonds offer the opportunity to significantly increase your own assets in a relatively short period of time. You also have this opportunity with larger companies that have already proven themselves on the market to still be involved, simply because they need liquidity again in the short term. As an investor, you then have the certainty that this company is stable, that it has good sales figures, that it has also established itself on the international market, and that you can invest directly in a company there. Ideally, you have direct contact with the company, and can also take a look at the company.

I personally love investor trips where I look at various investments with different investors and also have the opportunity to talk to the CEO on site and take a look at the whole company. I see how the team works together and can form an opinion directly because I get to know, feel, and assess the company up close.

Reto, let me jump in here for a moment because my whole business life is very much about travel and being in special places with extraordinary people; people that you would never get to know in their normal environment because you'd never get a meeting in their office. But because they also come to a place that is special to them, they are amazingly open to connecting. So, for me, that is something that the reader should really focus on. Bringing business and travel together to see and touch and feel the companies you want to invest in is one side of the story and certainly one of the best things you can do. But there is much more to these investor trips, as they all have the side effect of naturally connecting you with incredible people, and you never know what business opportunity will come next, just by being in the right place at the right time and meeting the right person. By traveling and attending special business events at the right time, I have met extraordinary people such as the former Vice President of Warner Brothers or the ex-CEO of Apple Computers, Europe. I have become friendly and on a first-name basis with those who manage one of the richest family fortunes in the world and many more.

I don't want to play the name-dropping game here, but what I want to say is that without traveling, my network would not include several 8- to even 12-figure business contacts. And all these people are now my friends! And of course, we add value to the lives of many others by doing good together. Without traveling—or let me rephrase that, by just staying in my office or at home—none of these connections would have been possible for me, and these relationships and what we do together makes a huge difference in my life and in the lives of many others. It made a difference *for life*, and I am so eternally grateful for that. That is why I like to say, "Connection is the new currency!"

I like this saying, Gisi, and let me mention another addition to the opportunity to invest in grown businesses - with convertible loans. Often, you need a good network that brings convertible loan deals on the table. They do not sell publicly but only in a network of a few selected people. That is why being connected through a network of other investors and your mentors is such a valuable thing. Sometimes, there is the great opportunity to combine different business models, and then it becomes extremely exciting for me as an investor.

CONNECTING
THE DOTS

Speed read: Connecting the dots, according to Steve Jobs, is only possible by looking at the past. In this chapter, which is a side brainstorming to the state of your Swiss Wealth Creation progress, we want to give you some impulses to learn how to connect the past with your future!

In Module 1, we talked about gold and silver, or more specifically, digital gold and silver as banking for freedom. Historically, we know some very valuable takeaways from the good old Gold Rush days. Let's travel back in time to the mid-19th century. It began in 1848 with the discovery of gold at Sutter's Mill in California, which triggered a massive influx of people seeking their fortune in gold mining. This event, known as the California Gold Rush, lasted until the early 1850s. The Gold Rush had a significant impact on the development of the American West and played a crucial role in shaping the history and economy of the United States during this period.

I want you to understand this: During the Gold Rush, it was not the miners who made the most profit. So, who were the richest people who made the most profits in the Gold Rush era? It makes a lot of sense to apply this lesson to the present day and see what plausible parallels there are.

Let's focus on the mid-19th century:

It's important to note that many different businesses that were only tangentially related to gold mining benefited from the Gold Rush; businesses like those that supplied digging tools and equipment. The Gold Rush also created opportunities for several other industries, such as transportation, hospitality, and banking, as the influx of people and wealth transformed the regions affected by the Gold Rush.

Companies that manufactured and supplied digging tools and equipment played a crucial role in supporting miners and profiting from the Gold Rush. Companies that manufactured pickaxes, an essential tool for digging and breaking rock, experienced high demand during the Gold Rush. These manufacturers saw increased sales as miners needed sturdy and reliable pickaxes for their mining activities. Shovels were another essential tool used by miners to move and sift through dirt and gravel in search of gold. Companies that manufactured shovels saw a surge in demand as miners needed durable and efficient shovels for their mining operations.

Mining equipment suppliers, which provided a range of mining equipment such as sluice boxes, rock crushers, and gold pans, were also in high demand during the Gold Rush. These suppliers catered to the needs of miners by providing specialized equipment to aid in the extraction and processing of gold.

Clothing and supply stores were in great demand as miners made their way to the gold fields. Do you know Levi's® jeans? —I bet you do! But you wouldn't know this global brand if the gold miners didn't need some proper pants! With so many miners in need of clothing and supplies, many businesses that sold clothing, boots, tents, food, and other essential items saw their sales increase as miners stocked up on supplies before heading to the gold fields.

Blacksmiths and metalworkers also played an important role in the Gold Rush, providing services such as tool repair, custom tool making, and metalworking for mining equipment. These skilled craftsmen benefited from the increased demand for their services during this time. Now ask yourself: *What is the next Gold Rush of today's world?* What are the trends that cannot be avoided in the next 3-5 years to 5 decades? And decide which companies are associated with these core trends, and which are the pick and shovel manufacturers, the equipment suppliers, the clothing brands and supply stores, and the blacksmiths and metalworkers of today's trends and tendencies.

Reto, I love the point you just made because I believe that the ability to connect the past and its patterns to the current situation and, from there, extend it into the future is the best thing a focused and purposeful investor can do.

Let me emphasize the word *purposeful* here. You know, there are these people who, just a few years ago, jumped like crazy into businesses they had no idea about. Like flies to the light, a lot of people jumped on the face mask bandwagon. Later on, they had no idea where to put the hundreds of thousands of these things they were sitting on, so let me just end this by saying that is the opposite of purposeful investing.

Right now, I am convinced that we are in the richest time ever. We live in a world that has more opportunities to create value than ever before. As long as we (oh, I really do not mean we, I mean *they*) can come out of the scarcity of minds, the world will have a tomorrow bliss that humanity is not even able to think of at the moment.

Imagine being able to invest in Levi's® Jeans in the mid-19th century, Apple in 1976, and Facebook in 2006.

There are many of these opportunities on my own table right now, and this is just my own very small and extremely reduced radar of what is possible globally.

Right Now!

Again, connection is the new currency, and when we connect, anything is possible. And I will tell you why right now:

I truly believe that the global crisis we are all going through has created a huge opportunity that only comes along once every 80 years.

I am 100% confident that we will be able to use this time of recreation to work together to create more value, more security, more peace of mind, and more freedom than ever before. Once again: Connection is the new currency—and being connected with the right personalities will be your key to all these accomplishments.

I will gladly show you how you can personally profit more from this time than you can imagine in your wildest dreams today, because the industrial, technological, and digital revolutions have already changed our world forever; now it is time for the revolution of meaning, courage, sovereignty, and humanity! I was talking about you becoming a purpose-driven investor. What this means for you is this:

You have the opportunity right now to learn how to align your business and investment decisions to take advantage of this global revolution. You are positioned right now to make a quantum leap in your wealth creation, and I know you are on the verge of your greatest breakthrough. I mean it, and I will go into great detail to tell you why:

They say your reputation is shaped by the crowd you run with. It is! I say your results are determined by the peer group you choose. They are, so choose wisely who you listen to!

Some make your day—others fake it away! Those of us who make it are definitely (still) in the minority, but we have the tools to change everything for you. Together with Reto and *The Swiss Wealth Creation* principles, I want to go far beyond what is possible by reading a great book. Think of *The Swiss Wealth Creation* as a door opener, and know our door is wide open. You just have to walk in. We're going to give you easy-to-implement strategies and systems that you can—and must-implement immediately to maneuver through this challenging time, because I believe this is the greatest opportunity the world has ever seen. Let me reframe that: This is the greatest opportunity *you* have ever seen. It is the opportunity of our lifetimes.

Let's face it: Yes, the world is a scary and very chaotic place right now. Yes, sure, that sounds like bad news, and yes, for many people it probably is. But where there is a big problem, there is also a big solution. And it is up to you which side you choose. So for you—assuming you choose the right side—it also means that the world is finally at the very important point in time that will enable your breakthrough. The great news is that the global shift has completely rearranged the business world and opened up new opportunities for all of us, right now, to create more profit, productivity and meaning in your life, and at the same time, more benefits, purposeful solutions, and partnerships that bring much more meaning to everyone else's lives. But let me tell you the crucial point: Only a handful of clever people will benefit from this massive change. You can be one of them.

What if you could use a system that allows you to consistently create your own independence and grow your business—no matter how big your successes already are—by a factor of 2, or much more? What would it mean to you to have 30-40% more investable capital available on demand, instantly, without having to work harder for it? You don't even have to scale your business. Scalability comes next. Is this leverage something you would definitely be interested in?

So, let's focus on multiplying your income and making you more recession and competition proof, especially in these uncertain times. That is what *The Swiss Wealth Creation* is all about. Understanding the real magic comes after you read this book, when you connect and implement what you can get if you want to. Because today is the time to rethink fast, to reinvent things, and to finally make what you've always wanted a reality.

And Reto and I will be absolutely honored and delighted to show you how.

Accepting that life will never be the same is the best way for you to move on to the great investments to come. If you learn to refocus and move fast enough, there is a lot of wealth coming your way. So, whether this new normal is good or bad for you depends on what you think, what you feel, what you decide to do, what you absolutely will not accept, and what you commit to in the next 2-6 months.

Whenever you hear those three words "the great reset"—and you will hear them around every corner—don't be afraid. Just get used to thinking and saying "no" to what is not in your best interest and know that we can create the *Greater Reset* when we have the right personalities coming together and the right people in the right positions. All of this can be inspired by this one book, and I believe it will be.

And I believe in you! I believe that billionaires will emerge from this global crisis, while other companies will quickly and painfully go bankrupt and disappear. The outcome is 100% up to you because you decide which side of the equation you want to be on.

How did you feel when, a few minutes earlier, you imagined yourself as an early-stage investor in Levi's, Apple, and Facebook? How would it feel for you to invest in the future of money, energy revolution, and growth spaces—for your next generations—*for* life? Just put the book down and allow yourself to dream and think about it. What will it mean for you and your family, what will it mean for your children and everyone else's children, if we connect and source the future with purposeful investments?

By leveraging disruptive industry breakthroughs, existing champions league-level business relationships, and three key forces, *The Swiss Wealth Creation System* can make this a reality for you. *With you!* The sky's the limit for your future. So, get ready and let's come together and innovate our way into an optimistic future. There are some trends that stand out in today's time of chaos and crisis:

- Current business models are obsolete. Most of the world's current businesses don't meet the needs of the digital age. Again: Linear thinking meets exponential times. Too many business leaders are not thinking about the social component. Too few companies are creating impact for life.
- Today's leadership is overwhelmed: The main problem with global leadership is the clumsy, awkward, slow, and graceless approach of governments.
- We don't see any government on earth that has the required entrepreneurial mindset. There is no commitment beyond the next election. There is no agility.
- Politicians are the last people in the world willing to take risks.
- To find solutions to the world's most important problems, we must embrace the entrepreneurial mindset.

- The world's problems demand engagement. They require us to be agile and willing to take risks. This means that the world's problems cannot be solved by governments. None of these are traits that politicians possess.

- But even the biggest problems can be solved: The world's problems, without exception, can be solved by solid, healthy, thoughtful companies. Now ask yourself one simple question: Why not yours? Let me change that question: Why not these purpose-driven businesses you are invested in?

Let me take you to that future and allow you to put aside the topic of hedging against inflation for the next 10 minutes or so. Let's dream and scheme now: I know you have a vision for a better future, and we're here to help you make it happen.

When was the last time you were truly amazed?

When was the last time you enjoyed life the most?

What was your greatest childhood or youth dream?

Is there something you love that you gave up for some reason; your children, your career, or your parents telling you to learn something decent? What if there was a way to make your dream come true, and as a direct result of living that dream, you could accelerate your business, your wealth, your successful investments, become authentic, and experience exponential growth on all levels?

Wouldn't that be great? This is the true meaning of what we are proposing with *The Swiss Wealth Creation.* Let's create a better future. Let's come together and create a Better Earth! Because we can all make a difference— and you better do it—before it's too late. It's the dreamers who take bold steps to create lasting, positive change and help make our world extraordinary again. The revolution of values is here, and now it's all about information and speed.

. . . .

> When I say the word *revolution,* the definition of revolution itself is "a group of individuals, united by a common goal, united by a common vision, in rebellion or revolt, against a common enemy or authority."—In this instance, that enemy or authority *is* the status quo!

. . . .

So, instead of looking for the next hopeful unicorn, we suggest you invest in a peaceful revolution — without fighting, but with sound monetary systems, and start to focus on the endless supply of free green energy that makes 100% self-sufficient living possible. Then we start the value creation dynamic in the areas of infrastructure, value added real estate, value added agriculture and, finally, we will have the necessary funds for what is the most important thought in your life: your dream! What is your dream? What would you do if you had the necessary resources to do what you want, now that you know the real offer of *The Swiss Wealth Creation* is not wealth — it is freedom!

Please be aware of everything you really, really want. Listen to your heart's desires, and let's make them a reality together. Because we can. To do so we will create and use…

THE CONSTANT CREATION OF
VALUE-CHAINS

Speed read: With each person who finds value in our work, and the more people involved who have a significant benefit from what we do, the likelihood of success increases exponentially!

Let's make it happen together and join forces to create an amazing future! In the best-selling book *World Unlocked*, I wrote the following section, which must be included in this book.

Most people are focused on the wrong problem. If you are frustrated with your circumstances, the problem is not with you. If you are unhappy with your business, then the problem doesn't lie within your company. Your problem lies with the systems you use. More specifically, your problem is within systems that others have made you believe will work, but that, in reality, don't. They simply can't. It is not the idea of the system to work for you. Quite the opposite.

I believe that the purpose of any business is to solve problems for other people or other businesses. What if we could rethink humanity along those lines, and make the future itself our key corporate purpose? Let us make the future our business. Because if we won't, very soon, we will have neither a business nor a future. My aim is to create value chains that benefit everyone. The more people involved who directly benefit from these undertakings, the more plausible and certain success becomes. Even in the noise of today's world, this is absolutely certain!

Moreover, I believe that the environment in which a company operates—whether that's the village, the country, or the state—should provide the company with the best possible conditions to fulfill the company's vision and mission. This means that politics and laws must ensure that companies can do their work under the most supportive conditions. That will help companies help others in the best possible way!

Politics, laws, and countries should help companies, and companies should help the people.

Tragically, today's world is the exact opposite. Politicians help broken industries by allocating billions of taxpayer dollars to bail out banks or subsidize sick ideas. Citizens pay industry through taxes, and industry helps politicians maintain their power. This is definitely a grievance that must be disrupted! Let's change directions by 180 degrees and begin building a new way.

Let's agree on one thing: as goal-oriented purposeful investors, we know that profit maximization is not limited to classical profit.

Profit is not only profit in the form of money, profit is the value of life - profit *for* life! Profit is security and safety. Profit is awareness, health, and well-being. Profit is the joy of life. Profit is natural regeneration, planting trees, etc. Now imagine that there is a way to invest your money that includes various multipliers and self-reinforcing mechanisms that allow the resources provided and the money generated to circulate in value chains and growing global cycles that become self-reinforcing.

For you, this means being part of an investment system that can be a profitable regenerative structure. An economic permaculture is a business concept with active developments for value creation, communities, economic spaces, and individual spaces to grow—for everyone who chooses to be a part of it.

Money circulates within the structure. Members can trade with other members within the group community without the money leaving the community space, and if you don't take money out, you don't pay taxes.

You may think this is too good to be true — and if you really believe that, you may be right. But if you believe that it is possible to create a Better Earth in every single moment, then you will want to quickly jump to the last chapter and see how you can get in touch with Reto and me so we can talk things through. You will get all the information you need to see that it is true, as it is the best thing you can do today to become a well-focused and purposeful *Swiss Wealth Creation* investor.

Thank you, Gisi. These thoughts are worth more than any gold and silver that money can buy.

Let us round this all up by adding a few final thoughts to the theme with which we began this brainstorming part of the book. The question was, what are the trends that cannot be avoided? And we wanted to identify those companies that are associated with core trends and tendencies.

During the Gold rush, the people who made the most money were not the lucky guys who found a few nuggets. The real winners were those who made all the accessories. Even today, there are opportunities, especially in gold and silver. And if you look carefully at life, you will see that there will most likely be a gold standard again. With precious metals in particular, you can invest directly in a mine, in which case you also have the risk of the mine— you have to know how well it is doing. But you also have the wonderful option of not investing directly in the mine, but in the next stage. In this case, that means the refinery.

The mines take the extracted rock, which hopefully contains a high percentage of gold and silver, to the refinery. But if one mine finds nothing, then no rock comes from there, while another mine finds a lot at the same time, then more rock comes from there.

But as an investor in a refinery, you benefit from a steady flow of rock coming into the refinery, and so you can also steadily increase your income, your value, because you are not dependent on the risk of the mining company.

These are the kinds of investment opportunities I like more and more. You will learn to appreciate these ideas because they will also lead you to learn to minimize risk again and again.

THE SWISS
DEALFLOW

Speed read: Individuals and companies seeking a safe haven for their assets know that Switzerland is the place to be! But there are Swiss Deals that only a few well-informed, smart investors know about. We want to introduce some of them in this chapter.

Switzerland has long been recognized as *the* place for trust and wealth protection due to its strong commitment to privacy, stability, and financial security. For many decades, the country's robust banking system, renowned for its discretion and reliability, has attracted individuals and businesses seeking a safe haven for their assets. Switzerland's political neutrality and long tradition of upholding confidentiality laws have further solidified its reputation as a trusted destination for wealth preservation. In addition, the Swiss legal system, known for its integrity and efficiency, provides a solid foundation for protecting assets and ensuring the enforcement of contracts. With its combination of financial expertise, political stability, and a culture of trust, Switzerland continues to be the preferred choice when it comes to protecting your wealth and preserving your values.

But let's break new ground here. You know how I feel about banks—including Swiss banks—and you remember that I want you to become your own bank. One of the following investment opportunities can do this for you like few others.

There are some really great options that the average person doesn't even know about. A very typical Swiss product, for example, is balsamic vinegar in oak barrels that is stored in the glaciers of the Swiss Alps. This is certainly something that I believe you, dear reader, are not yet familiar with. It is only used here as an example. As an in-depth illustration of the possibility of focusing on some very valuable commodities that the very rich buy, I want to broaden your horizons, especially to get you thinking about investing in such assets.

I want to tell you why I think investing in assets that the rich use is a great plan: There is a trend of increasing wealth concentration among the richest individuals during times of crisis, and this can be attributed to several factors. First, during periods of economic downturn, such as the 2008 global financial crisis or the events of 2020 till today, governments and central banks implement measures to stabilize the economy and support financial markets. On one hand, it increases inflation, but the other side of the coin is that quantitative easing and low interest rates tend to benefit asset owners; in other words, the richest individuals get even richer. Second, crises often lead to market dislocations and economic restructuring, which can create opportunities for the wealthy to acquire distressed assets at lower prices. This allows them to expand their wealth and investment portfolios while others may be forced to sell assets at a discount.

In addition, the wealthiest individuals often have diversified investment portfolios that are not solely dependent on traditional industries. In times of crisis, certain sectors may decline significantly, while others, such as technology and healthcare, may thrive. The wealthy tend to have investments in these resilient sectors, allowing them to benefit from their growth even in difficult times.

Whether this is good or not, you have to answer for yourself. What I want for you is that, very soon, you are one of those rare few who become richer and richer. So, for now, let's stay with the consequences. As more rich people get richer, more of their wealth has to be invested in financial assets or intangible assets.

Do you need the most expensive vinegar in the world? No, I think you can make wonderful meals with a good standard vinegar from the grocery store. But will the richest buy the most expensive vinegar they can get? Definitely, yes, because they can. And that is why I think you should take advantage of these dynamics; it is just a choice. It's *your* choice to get a slice of the potential profits from the choices the richest make.

If we stay with balsamic vinegar, the small barrels are stored in ice for over ten years and then sold to exclusive clients and kitchens of five-star restaurants. There are lucrative investment opportunities hidden in Swiss ice, and anyone is invited. When you want to, you can even see it for yourself; you are flown into the mountains by helicopter, and you can see it directly in the glacier. For me, there are also these experiences, the investments-events that make the whole thing even more interesting. Also here, again, imagine what exciting people you will meet on a helicopter flight over that glacier.

These are all things that you will learn to invest in when you choose *The Swiss Wealth Creation* path. These are investment opportunities that no bank will give you, no insurance company will give you, and no financial advisor will give you, because they simply don't have these nuggets in their portfolio or on their radar. They are not even thinking about these incredible opportunities—so what I want to tell you is this: These are opportunities that you're not really going to find in the marketplace. And these niche products often have extraordinary returns precisely because they are not mainstream. If you don't like balsamic vinegar, you can do the same thing with rum or whiskey or wine. There are many ways to acquire assets such as these that the ultra-rich are eager to buy when you are following the Swiss model.

TRADING
OPERATIONS

Speed read: Generating cash flow through trading projects can be beneficial for several reasons. First, trading projects allow for the generation of immediate income. By identifying and acquiring projects that have the potential for quick turnaround and profitability, you can generate cash flow in a relatively short period of time.

When you invest in cash flow projects, it's important that you get a regular flow of money back. Of course, this is very important when you are just starting to invest. But even for experienced investors, it is extremely important that there is always a flow of free money coming back to you. You don't want all your money to be tied up somewhere over the years, but you also want a certain amount of liquidity, which is why these projects are a very important part of *The Swiss Wealth Creation* setup.

Again, there are different types of projects, and we will only scratch the surface in this book.

Project trading can provide diversification and flexibility in your investment portfolio. By trading projects, you can spread your risk across different industries and sectors, reducing your exposure to single projects or markets. Your diversification can help mitigate potential losses and improve your overall portfolio performance. In addition, when you learn how to use project trading, it can provide opportunities for capital appreciation. By identifying undervalued projects and selling them at a higher price, you can realize capital gains and increase your overall wealth. This can be particularly beneficial in markets where there is a high demand for certain types of projects, or a shortage of supply with often no income taxes on capital gains. (Check this point with your tax advisor; every country might be different.)

Trading projects allows you to take advantage of market inefficiencies and mispriced assets. As soon as you grow in your expertise and market knowledge, you will be able to identify projects that are undervalued or overlooked by others, acquire them at a bargain price, and then sell them for a profit.

Of course, there are risks involved, from market volatility to regulatory challenges and project-specific uncertainties. Therefore, thorough due diligence and careful analysis are critical when you engage in project trading to maximize the potential benefits and minimize the associated risks.

But as you learn all the necessary basics, cash flow through trading projects will become a viable strategy for you to generate immediate income, diversification, capital appreciation, and the ability to take advantage of market inefficiencies.

Again, the focus is always on the questions: "Where is the money coming from?", "How do I get that regular return?", and "How is all the value created?" That's where financial education comes in again - making sure you know how the profit is generated. Let's stay with this financial literacy for a moment: If we look at the fact that, in Switzerland, we have an official inflation of about 3 percent right now—in Germany, it is about 8 to 9 percent—these are the official figures. If I look at my expenses, from the grocery store to gasoline and energy costs, then I assume that this is an average of 10 to 15 percent, or even 10 to 20 percent. This is the real inflation that is there at the moment; every year you can look at your bills and you will agree. That means that you also must have assets that give you a 10 or 20 percent return on your investment. That means that your money needs to continue to grow at 10 to 20 percent or it is fading away (like banks).

One of the pillars that I want you to learn about is the one that contains all these projects that are out there that are not being promoted by the banks and the insurance companies, because they often mistakenly promote the idea that anything that yields more than 5 or 6 percent is a high-risk project. I wrote about that misconception in the beginning of the book. So, I want to talk about a couple of possible types of projects, why companies offer them, and how you can get involved.

One possibility is retail projects, where a company buys retail products and—just as one example—sells them through Amazon. All of these transactions are usually financially capped. That means that at some point as the company gets bigger, they run out of cash and look for ways to bring more money in. In this particular case, they then sell some of the goods that they already have in stock on Amazon to investors. There is a service agreement that allows them to resell the products through their channel, and you get a share of the profit that they make. That's nice! No workload and you get benefits from the work of others. And remember: it is a real asset, not a financial product.

Again, focus on the questions: "Where is the money coming from?" and "What is their added value?" The added value is clearly that they can buy cheaper because they have more mass. That means they can drive the purchase price down further; they have a higher margin and, therefore, they can give you very good returns. I think you can see why it's important to have a clear and plausible understanding of where the value is created. Typically, they buy the products with a margin of 300 to 600 percent; a significant part of that margin still goes to Amazon, but there is a lot left over and you can participate in that business—without any workload! So, the larger the purchase quantities, the lower the purchase price and the higher the margin on the selling price. This is one of the projects in the area of trade, only to give you an example. Please note that in this book we can only give you examples, and we do so from an eagle's eye perspective. If I were to show you actual investment opportunities on my desk, they would have disappeared and been replaced by others, maybe even better ones, by the time this book is published. And who knows, maybe you will get the book years after its release: Even then we will have an excellent Swiss Dealflow on our tables, but you will only get these nuggets when we connect in the moment that is yours to invest. Read the last chapter when the moment is right and then—AND ONLY THEN—we will be happy to give you some real deals that are the right deals for you at the right time. I promise.

So please don't be frustrated that I'm only scratching the surface here when it comes to actual investment opportunities. These cannot be conveyed through a book. And when we are talking about that: You know I could easily teach you in 3 to 7 days about every single chapter in this book. It is not our idea to give you in-depth mastery with this edition; our wish is to get your mind and investors' engine started. We will be there for your financial empowerment when your best moment for that journey has come. And you will know where to find us. Besides education, our main goal for you is that you get started! We don't want to sell education; we want *you* to be an action taker.

Please also be aware and remember that we can't, won't, and don't want to help everyone. Of course, we screen and select our clients very carefully—but if you are a perfect fit for us, we will only find out when you contact us. And when you are a perfect fit, then you have an extraordinary future ahead of you, I can guarantee that right now.

So let's find out, always at the right time. We look forward to connecting with you—right now, when this is YOUR moment: Skip to the latest chapter and follow what we suggest there.

So now you learned about a retail example of project trading. Another part of the projects goes into the area of infrastructure projects. In these projects, as an investor, you buy part of an infrastructure, a company, and here too you work with a service contract. The company makes a profit, and you share in this profit.

Why do companies do this? There is often a scenario where companies are not getting loans from banks; for example, in the medical cannabis sector. And that's why they often look for the opportunity to go to the private investor market, to sell certain assets directly and then give the owner a share of the sales that are made with those assets. For example, you can buy a certain number of plants of medical cannabis, plants that are grown under the strictest conditions; the crop is sold, and you get a share of the profits. The advantage for these companies is that they are stronger in the market, they can continue to grow, and they are no longer dependent on banks as financiers. The advantage for you is that you have a short period of time to get the returns and you can create cash flow without doing any work. We have many of these projects following our Swiss model—all of which are only here for a short window of time. So, let's find out which window is wide open for you when it's your time. Make sure these windows close again - money loves speed. Do not wait to get in front of the curve.

I would also like to at least mention the next point. This is also about the capabilities of a company that is already large and wants to grow further. Here, too, there are sometimes liquidity bottlenecks. Then something called Bridge Lending is often a way to continue. This means that they go to the private market and borrow money for a certain period of time—three, six, or twelve months, or as much as two or three years—depending on the project. Typically, what happens in the real estate sector is that they buy a property that they can renovate and then refinance and resell, and that's why Bridge Lendings are often possible in that three-to-twelve-month range.

Another thing is ownership, which means that you take a direct stake in a company and usually share in the annual profits. This could be, for example, a coffee or cocoa farm that wants to buy another farm, so the company itself owns more farms, makes the new company grow again, and manages the whole farm; and because you own part of the company, you are also involved in the profits of the company.

Now, I imagine you are reading this and wondering if there is a lot of coffee and cocoa in Switzerland. No, there is not. But as you know, we Swiss have a huge chocolate industry that gives us tier-1 connections to many cocoa farms around the world, and you may also know that we have iconic Lila cows in Switzerland. You may have heard of Milka, a Swiss brand of chocolate owned by Mondelez International. The company is known for its Alpine milk chocolate and Lila Cows, which are made with Swiss milk.

Believe it or not, it is possible to use the same model and become a co-owner in Swiss cows on the "Alm" (alpine pasture) and get a significant return in Swiss milk production.

Your investment could involve buying shares in a cooperative, which then builds an agricultural facility, and then you have a share in the profits that go back into it. There are wonderful developments in Germany and the Czech Republic with regenerative cooperatives that can create assets like healthy soil. Creating healthier agriculture is very important for our future, and these are aspects that we need to keep in mind as well-focused, purposeful *Swiss Wealth Creation* investors.

One of the most exciting projects in recent years for me are the so-called out-of-the-box projects. These are mainly known only to very large, institutional investors and are completely unknown to private individuals.

For example, live settlements, which are US life insurance policies in the secondary market that large insurance companies and large banks have in their portfolios.

And here, too, there are now opportunities to participate with small amounts of money and not buy an entire life insurance policy, but just a portion of it, and then participate in it again when it matures and flows back in that way.

This is not a special Swiss opportunity—quite the opposite—and what that means for you is that this is certainly a less predictable option than the previous ones, but it can be very lucrative when the returns come.

And again, my idea for this part of our journey is to give you some ideas from the eagle's perspective. We can only talk about specific possibilities individually and in direct contact.

THE HIDDEN GEM:
AGRICULTURE

Speed read: Investing in agriculture puts you at the beginning of the value chain. The earlier you are in the value chain, the higher your margin. You supply a socially essential commodity—everyone needs eating and drinking—and you generate cash flow with high returns.

Another huge area of opportunity lies in all the agricultural investment opportunities around the world. This is certainly something that will be increasingly in demand in the future, as the explosion in the number of people on earth means that more and more food will be needed. That's why there are an increasing number of projects in the agricultural sector.

There are many ways to get involved in a farming project. For example, you can buy a piece of land with a service contract on it, which means that you are the owner of the land and everything on the land. These material goods belong to you. You are registered as the owner in the land registry, and you have a service contract with a service provider who will provide the agricultural services on that land for you. That could be cows for milk or a vineyard. Or—if you look at it more globally—it can be orange trees planted on the land and managed by a service provider. So, whoever is growing the products on your farmland is selling the harvest and involving you in all the monetization that comes out of it. There are a lot of exciting, long-term projects in agriculture.

They can be citrus fruits, walnut trees, or persimmon trees; in other words, they can be focused on a specific agricultural product, but they can also be general investments in agricultural cooperatives. There is a very wide range of possibilities for you as an investor. Again, the question is *why*? Why are farmers doing this? It is also about growth. They want to continue to grow their businesses, but again, there are limits to what they can do alone, and they solve their liquidity problems by selling outright parts of the new land that they want to buy, and then they just focus on their core business, which is the actual farming, so that you as an investor can participate in that business.

Reto, I have learned that there is a very special security backup, especially in agriculture—and I find that very interesting: A great side effect of farming is that you invest in a piece of land, a plantation, or even a coop. Of course, it's about the crop, but the security itself is the land! The land that you buy to farm that belongs to you is the security backup I'm talking about. Land cannot be multiplied at will and therefore it retains its value, even more so than real estate. Real estate can be built up, and it will continue to go up for quite some time, but land is really limited, and that's what makes these investments so valuable worldwide. When you invest in land, the net asset value of the land alone can go up six to eight percent a year. I am connected to projects in South America where the Bioceano Route is being built. This is a land route that will have a similar economic impact as the Panama Canal. Even without this new link between the Atlantic and the Pacific, which will connect the two extremes of the South American continent from Brazil to Chile in an unprecedented way, the value of land in the region I am talking about has increased by six to eight percent *every* year—and this over the last 30 years—so imagine what happens to your investment when you buy agricultural land in a part of the world that has all the requirements to become the fastest growing economic area of an entire continent. That in itself is a good investment, but you want to have productive capital. You want to produce something on your land. You want something to grow there.

But the best is yet to come... so, pay especially close attention!

QUANTUM SAFE TOKENIZED AGRICULTURE

Reto, do you know what Liquid Gold is? I just had an incredible call with my North American partner, and the topic we discussed is groundbreaking. I'm thrilled to announce that we will soon launch the first-ever quantum-proof Real-World Asset (RWA) token for a very special agricultural project. Imagine being part of it—no matter where you are—and benefiting from innovations like this cutting-edge rainforest honey, known for its healing properties and referred to as "Liquid Gold" by the Maya. And all this at the touch of a button. There are unique bees, revered as gods in Mayan culture, that produce this extraordinary honey, which is literally sold at a price comparable to gold. The price for 10 ml is around $30.

This is not typically a Swiss topic. However, we aim to have integrated a Swiss company into the value creation chain, specializing in Better Earth endeavors worldwide and bringing trust to a vetted circle of projects. So, even if a production is based in the land of the Mayans, or on the Canary Islands, or elsewhere, you don't have to venture into the rainforests to benefit from it...

Now, with Web3 technology, we are not only creating a highly innovative approach that will set this brand apart and enhance trust and security for our customers, we are also pioneering the use of quantum-resistant cryptography in agriculture. This, I believe, is one of the most significant breakthroughs of our time. And it is exactly what Reto and I call a New Era of Investment! It opens up a world of opportunities pivoting from the old world—taking energy—to the new: Giving energy, creating freedom.

Let's keep it simple for now: Quantum-resistant cryptography is designed to withstand attacks from quantum computers, which are far more powerful than classical computers and could potentially break today's encryption algorithms. By using this advanced cryptography, we ensure the security and integrity of our agricultural projects. Tokenization is the process of converting a physical asset into a digital token. Experts predict that asset tokenization will reach $16 trillion by 2030, revolutionizing asset financing. Major financial institutions, including Goldman Sachs, Citigroup, BlackRock, and JP Morgan, are already embracing blockchain technology to streamline their operations and lead the adoption of tokenization in finance.

Investing in projects like hydroponic agriculture or the Mayan "Liquid Gold" is not only a perfect counterbalance to bad practices like genetic modification by companies like Monsanto, but using tokenization in recreative agriculture also represents the most precious hidden gem in the world of investing. Join us in recreating our future with intelligent solutions and be part of this exciting journey!

So, agriculture is one of the most magical assets you can have. You are at the very beginning of value creation. You do good for a lot of people. The more people that are involved, the more value you create, and you can bring lots of people together to create a huge amount of value.

Remember: Connection is the new currency!

SPECIAL INFRA-STRUCTURE PROJECTS

Speed read: Investing in specialized infrastructure projects is a great idea due to growing demand, resilience, long-term contracts, diversification benefits, potential for value-added strategies, and alignment with environmental concerns!

Especially in real estate, partnerships are a big deal: Find a real estate partner that thinks outside the box, such as seller financing, to build a portfolio with a minimum of equity.

In the area of infrastructure projects, I would like to address two further possibilities. One is in the area of storage. Storage, which has grown very strongly, in the USA in particular, over the last few decades, is also increasingly coming to Europe because people are becoming more flexible, are moving more than they used to, have more things that they can't or don't want to part with, and are looking for storage space where they can store things temporarily, with the idea of storing them for one, two or three months. In most cases, everything is stored for years, and because the prices for these storage units are relatively low, it doesn't affect the budget that much, and these are usually very, very long-standing customers. So, if you can buy a warehouse there - for example, through a franchise system - buy an entire warehouse and rent out all the storage compartments. That's also a very nice cash flow project that generates monthly cash flow once it's up and running and a large part of it is rented out.

So, investing in niche infrastructure projects such as storage facilities can be a compelling opportunity for several reasons. Here are a few key points for you:

1) **Growing demand:** Demand for storage facilities is on the rise due to various factors such as the growth of e-commerce, urbanization, and changing consumer behavior. As the need for warehousing and logistics solutions increases, investments in storage facilities can tap into this growing demand.

2) **Resilience and stability:** Storage facilities tend to be resilient and stable, even during economic downturns. They are considered essential infrastructure, providing a critical link in the supply chain for various industries. This resilience can help mitigate risk and provide a stable income stream for you.

3) **Long-term contracts:** Storage facilities often operate under long-term leases with tenants, providing a very predictable and steady cash flow for you. These contracts typically have built-in rent

escalations, ensuring potential income growth over time.

4) **Diversification:** Investing in storage facilities can provide diversification benefits to your investment portfolio. It provides exposure to the real estate sector while tapping into the growing demand for logistics and warehousing solutions driven by broader trends such as e-commerce and supply chain optimization.

5) **Potential for value-added strategies:** Warehousing facilities offer opportunities for value-added strategies, such as improving operational efficiencies, expanding, or repositioning existing facilities, or incorporating technological advancements. These strategies can improve the overall performance and value of the investment.

6) **Environmental considerations:** With the increasing focus on sustainability and environmental responsibility, investing in storage facilities that incorporate energy-efficient technologies or renewable energy sources can align with these trends and attract environmentally conscious tenants.

Now, the second opportunity I want to share with you related to infrastructure projects is in real estate. Again, there are many, many opportunities. I could probably give you a week's worth of useful knowledge on every paragraph of this very condensed chapter. So, always remember, this book is written from an eagle's eye view of your future as a successful investor. Let's go into detail together when you're ready and we both feel it's right for you.

Nine out of ten millionaires became millionaires through real estate. For example, you can build a portfolio of single-family homes by maximizing their value. You can build some of them from scratch or, depending on your budget, buy fixer-uppers, renovate them, and then refinance or sell them. There are different types of properties you can buy. Something I really like to do is to work closely with an experienced realtor, a top real estate agent who thinks out of the box like I do and uses what's called a seller financing model: This means that I don't need external financing from a bank, but I tell the seller, "Look, I'll buy your property from you, but you finance it for me".

Let me explain this shortly: Seller financing in real estate is when the person selling a property, such as a house or piece of land, helps you as the buyer by providing a loan to purchase the property. Instead of you going to a bank or lender to get a loan, the seller becomes the lender and offers to finance the purchase himself. Let's say you want to buy a house, but you don't have enough money to pay for it all at once. The seller, the person selling the house, can say, "Hey, I can help you buy this house by giving you a loan. You can pay me back over time, just like you would with a bank loan." This means that instead of getting a loan from a bank, you make regular payments directly to the seller. You and the seller agree on things like the interest rate, the length of time to pay off the loan, and the amount of money to be paid each month.

This sort of financing, which is also not commonly known, can be helpful for you when you do not qualify for a traditional bank loan—or when you just don't want to work with a bank—because you want more flexibility in the terms of the loan.

It can also be beneficial for the seller who wants to sell the property quickly, or who wants to earn extra income from the interest on the loan. So, with this seller financing, you can pay back to the seller a portion every month, and at the end, there is a balloon payment - a final payment. And for you as an investor, this means that you only have to get involved in the deal with perhaps 10 percent of the sales price, and the rest is financed directly by the seller.

Again, it makes sense for you as an investor to understand the why. Why should a seller take out seller financing in the first place? There can be several reasons. On the one hand, it could be that he doesn't need the money quickly and would like to have slightly higher profits in the long term. On the other hand, there may be tax reasons, because when he sells this property, he may pay a large amount of tax on it. However, with seller financing, it may be possible for him to spread the entire tax burden over several years because only a certain part of the income arrives in his account each month.

Experience has shown me that many sellers are not even aware of this model. It takes a certain amount of empathy on the part of the realtor to make this option appealing to the seller. But in most cases, after a while, the sellers say, "Wow, that's brilliant!" because they understand they don't pay the tax on the sale immediately.

They understand that they as sellers have a regular income. A regular income, which means they don't have to worry about immediately investing a large amount of money from the sale themselves, but they have sold their property, receive a regular, solid payment into their account every month, and the whole thing is secured by their own property, which they also know the value of. And since everything is set up properly in the contract, they also know that their loan is well secured.

In addition, he knows that a regular income will come in because he knows the property and is aware, from renting it out, what the rental income is or can be. He knows what rent can be charged for it. This is a business model with many, many positive characteristics. Once you know this very well, you will also find the right sellers. As I said, mainly sellers who want to sell in a tax-optimized way, sellers who don't want to have to deal with large sums of money, and sellers who are also keen to have a regular income from the property, which they also know themselves, but no longer have to or want to have the responsibility of owning their own property.

So it's a very, very exciting way for you to build up a passive income with as little equity as possible when you find the right seller. It is well worth it to focus on finding the right one for these kinds of special infrastructure projects. I will be happy to help.

As an aside, I just had a conversation yesterday with a contact from Texas who has been very successful in real estate. He is now retiring from his own company at the age of 70, and his company typically buys apartment complexes of 400 to 600 units. People like this contact of mine are especially excited about the opportunity to take their businesses to the next stage—or in this case, to the next important stage in their lives—with seller financing. And I am always happy to share my contacts with you when you would like to get into this very interesting category as well. It's an investment area where you can create a lot of wealth with relatively little effort, and that's what we want for you!

Yes, Reto, that is exactly what we want. I get up every day with the drive to create a better earth for as many people as possible, and that starts with the desire of every single person involved to take full responsibility for their own lives. I believe it would be great to have a brainstorming session based on what you shared right now, and at this point, have a glance at special infrastructure projects that are only possible in Switzerland!

Oh, there are several possibilities that come immediately to mind, Gisi. First, vegetables. We grow a lot of vegetables here in Switzerland. That would be one possibility. But typically, the "Alm" would be the place to start brainstorming — the Swiss alpine pastures, of course. There are a lot of farms — alpine huts. You go up to the Alps in the summer and you're way up in nature there, far away from all the noise, the mainstream, the fake media, distraction, traffic, and pollution.

Yes, I believe that alone will become a business opportunity. Having the right places to BE!

Yes, Gisi, and it would also be something where we could consider buying or leasing certain farms in the Swiss Alps and then renting them out or making the livestock available. I can assure you it will be very exciting to look at. Probably the next idea will be a game changer. What I have in mind are some of the safest places in the world: Right inside our Swiss mountains.

Known for their robust security measures, these facilities are often used to store valuable assets such as gold, precious metals, and important documents. One notable example is the Swiss Gold Vault, located in the Swiss Alps. This vault is known for its state-of-the-art security systems and strict access controls. It is designed to withstand a variety of threats, including physical attacks, natural disasters, and even nuclear events. The exact details of the security measures used in these facilities are kept confidential to maintain their effectiveness. But what I can tell you is that they are drilled many miles into the solid rock of the mountains.

So, the Swiss Alps themselves can be a huge investment opportunity if you have the right connections—what you so wisely call "the new currency," Gisi—and their remote and mountainous terrain alone provides an extra layer of protection and seclusion for vaults and bunkers, and your wealth.

The Swiss government has established strict regulations and oversight to ensure the integrity and security of these facilities. They are subject to regular inspections and audits to maintain the highest security standards. It is important to reiterate that the specific details and access to these vaults and bunkers are typically restricted to authorized personnel and clients, and the confidentiality and security of the stored assets are of the utmost importance.

Since the Swiss Alps are naturally home to high-security vaults, bunkers, and depots that provide a safe and protected environment for the storage of numerous valuable assets, you can definitely think about owning your own piece of the Alps! I am almost certain that there are several unused structures that are privately owned and therefore available for purchase. And just like the facilities that already exist, these structures are covered by some of the strongest mountain fortifications in the world. And while I don't yet know how we're going to make this a huge success and what the details will be, I'm sure we'll be able to buy some very special assets somehow. It's not farming anymore, it's just in the mountains, and you can own the massive structure to perfectly secure wealth for yourself and others.

YOUR HOME IS
NOT YOUR ASSET

Speed read: You must take your home out of the equation. It is not an investment; it is a liability. Learn to provide homes for other people and you will increase your wealth.

Real estate is a topic I could write numerous books about, but there are thousands of books on the market already, so I only want to touch on a few points. What I found very interesting is that in a broader perspective, there are many more opportunities in real estate than just owning your own home. For some of them, it's hard to believe they are categorized real estate, but they are worth at least having a look at.

You have already read about agriculture, seller financing, real estate, and warehousing. Here are some more ideas: One thing I often see when I talk to clients is that they have real estate in their name—real estate they do not fully own, by the way—and then usually only a small portion. When I look deeper, I see that most of their wealth is in that one piece of real estate, which is often their own home, but:

Robert Kiyosaki is famous for this saying!

....

"Your home is not your asset."

....

What he means is that an asset puts money in your pocket. And a liability takes money out of your pocket. And your own home just takes money out of your pocket, unless you have a studio in your home that you can rent out, then it puts a little money back in your pocket.

As an investor, you should ideally have about 30% of your total assets in real estate, and you should even have it in more than one property for diversification. So, if you have real estate in your name, make a calculation to see how much of your total assets are in your real estate. I bet it will be more than 80% in most cases! And that can be considered a high risk.

Many real estate millionaires do not own a home but rent an apartment. Why do they do this? I see several reasons:

Instead of putting their own money into their own real estate, they let it work in areas with higher returns and rent an apartment with some of those returns. They have the flexibility of the assets and still have some returns available even after paying the rent. Here's an example:

You can buy a $1 million house with $200,000 of your own money and $800,000 in bank loans at 5%, which leaves you with annual expenses of 40,000. Or you can put 200,000 in an investment at 12%. That gives you 24,000 per year. Instead of spending 40,000, you earn 24,000, which is 64,000 more in your pocket. If you divide this by 12 months, you get 5,333 per month. If you spend only half of that on an apartment, you will have one of the best apartments in the city to rent!

Another point is that when you buy your own home, you usually want to have the highest standard. So you buy the most expensive items for your kitchen, bathroom, and living room. With some cheap money from the bank for your mortgage loan, this is an easy financing.

Reto, you just made such an important point, and I couldn't agree more. I lived for years in a millionaire's environment with houses that were like museums— every one of them; most of them empty of life. Even without looking at their books, this family had a very good cash cow business, and the surplus went into very luxurious homes. And these homes (I bet like you) have more than 80% of their assets locked up.

And they loaded it up to the roof with the most precious items for interior and exterior decoration. I have been sitting on a black porcelain throne with gold trim from Milan, Italy, for about 7 years. Other houses were opulent, filled with pink marble and incredible furniture. But when the head of the family wanted to sell these houses, no one wanted to pay the price because the taste was really "unique", so years went by, and the houses were not sold.

It doesn't make much difference whether you're a multimillionaire or not: Don't tie up too much wealth in the house you live in; and if you're going to sell a multimillion dollar property, it's best to keep the interior very basic and ask the buyer what they like—and when you know it, make it real—rather than stuffing the mansion with all the objects *you* love and then trying to find the one in a million that matches your own "high class taste". It's like going fishing, putting your favorite cake on the hook, and waiting for it to be desired.

Most of these family members I write about have had to work hard all their lives—weekends included! Instead of putting all those millions into real estate, which really provides a great income without being a 24/7 workaholic, they just had a huge load of luxury homes that did not bring in a dime for years. There would have been so many better opportunities for them.

Reto, this is what you remind me of when you talk about people's responsibility for their homes. Maybe that is why I love renting beautiful places and having the freedom to leave them behind when an even more beautiful place comes along.

Yes, Gisi, in my words, your own home is just another expenditure of money that increases your liabilities, and an even smaller part of your home belongs to you; only your liabilities are growing.

Many say it increases the value of their home when they put in expensive kitchens or amazing furniture. True, if they want to sell it now. But if they want to sell it in a few years, the value goes down pretty quickly. Most of the depreciation happens in the first few years after the investment, so it is not really an increase in value.

Even if it is your home, you usually have a lot of emotion invested in it. This can cause you to not make the financial decision that is best for your financial future. A beautiful garden can cost a lot of money and make you happy. Is it financially wise to invest such a large amount of money in your garden? I leave it up to you to decide.

Last point here - you will always have recurring costs for your heating, roof, solar, windows, facade, etc., as long as you put some money aside on a regular basis, either by your bank through your amortization plan and/or by yourself, that is always money leaving your pocket instead of putting money into your pocket.

Never forget what made Las Vegas great: The house always wins! In our context, remember from now on:

The bank always wins!

Sometimes my wife Conny and I discuss whether we should have bought our own home 25 years ago. During that time, of course, we paid a lot of rent. And with the increase in real estate values here in Switzerland, we would have made a good capital gain. Would we be willing to sell this house? I do not know. So, we have an increased value of our house, but we are still all tied up in it. After a full cost calculation, I am convinced that we would have done much better to rent and invest instead of tying up our funds in a mortgage plan.

I urge you to realize how much of your home is really "your" home, and for the other part, you have only the liability but not the asset.

Your bank is a big winner, with no liability but the right to the asset if you cannot pay.

WORKING WITH
TRUSTED
PARTNERS
FUNDS AND
CROWDFUNDING

Speed read: I like to work with specialists in each field rather than doing it all myself.

You will like that, too — there are real estate funds where you can make a nice profit while someone else does the work!

If you rent and still want to invest in real estate, there are other options. And here is my first nugget when it comes to real estate:

- Make sure you work with a trustworthy partner, and make sure the fund is backed by the property. There are many pitfalls, so the decision plan is very important.

- Working with a trusted partner who has a good track record and a portfolio of valuable properties can be a great way to diversify your portfolio. Do your due diligence on the partner you are working with and the projects they are working on.

- You also need to be aware that you are a partial owner or sometimes even an investor in a financial product, such as a tracker certificate or an actively managed certificate. If these instruments are backed by real estate, then you can profit from these real estate deals.

- Another common thing that has popped up in the last couple of years is crowdfunding. In real estate, there are a lot of platforms that offer these deals.

Again, it is very important to know who is behind the platform, what the deals are, what the track record is, what the liabilities are, and what the risk/reward is.

STAY & STORE: MOBILE HOME STORAGE AND SELF-CHECK-IN HOTEL

Speed read: Convenient Living is a trend. As an investor, it must be a daily routine to look at the problems that humanity has and the possible solutions that an investor can provide...

... and if you go one step further, look at the same situation 3 to 5 years from now. If you can start now to provide solutions to problems that people will have in 3 to 5 years, you will create a goldmine.

Let me give you some examples: we talked earlier about storage solutions. Another example is mobile homes. Since 2021, the number of mobile homes has increased dramatically. When I talk to mobile home owners, there is a common problem and that is: "Where can I park my motorhome when I am not using it?" — There are no parking lots! So, if you have the money and the connections, why not either build a mobile home storage hall, or rent an unused factory hall and convert it into a mobile home storage hall? RV owners pay a good rent for a safe place to store their beloved vehicles. And if you add a few security and utility gadgets like 24/7 video surveillance, heating/cooling controls, a wash station, and an RV shop, you can even raise your rents.

With digitization comes the experience of using digital tools. One thing that has gotten a lot of traction is self-check-in hotels. This is another great opportunity for a real estate cash-cow.

The hotel guest does all the work himself; no staff is needed at the front desk, and human power, such as a cleaning staff, is limited to the minimum. All other services can be outsourced to a 24/7 operator and maintenance. You can run such a facility from home and only need to be in the facility for very limited hours.

FUTURE
REAL ESTATE
FOR RENT

Speed read: As an investor, it must be a daily routine to look at the problems that humanity has and the possible solutions that an investor can provide...

Let's say you want to invest in traditional real estate. Do your best research - what are the future problems, and what solutions can you provide?

People often want to rent something luxurious and expensive to make more profit. However, in my experience, it is usually the cheap rents that make the most profit. I learned this when I invested in US real estate. At first, I could not imagine investing in a low asset property. But after buying the first house for under $20,000 and making a decent profit, I finally saw the opportunity. My coach told me to look at the market.

Low budget rentals have a much larger number of interested people than luxury rentals. And the return on investment is usually much greater. The only downside is you sometimes have to deal with a different type of people, so you can work with a specialist who is used to working with them.

What is one of the problems facing future generations? Lack of money. So, they will have to save on rent and be willing to live in different types of housing than they do today. Shared living will be a niche that will grow, like having your room in a big apartment and sharing the living room and kitchen. Or, if you are near a university, there are a lot of young people who want to rent an apartment but cannot afford to rent on their own. So you can offer a 5-room apartment for 5 people, each paying more than 1/5 of the total cost. Or you can divide that one apartment into 3 small apartments.

If you go into start-ups, one of their problems is that they do not know how fast their business will grow or in which direction. So why not offer them a month-to-month rent that is higher than if they have a one-year notice period? Also, pop-up stores are something new, and if you can offer space to rent, you can have a very profitable business model. Again, you need to know the market and work with the right people.

We at WGW-Advisors are connecting those opportunities with investors looking to get something started. You can reach my office at support@wgw-advisors.com and let my team know what opportunity you are interested in.

ASSETIZATION
MADE IN
SWITZERLAND

Speed read: We know that there are different types of investment personalities. For testing the waters of inflation protection without really unbanking yourself, assetization may be for you.

You may want to see this chapter as a "P.S."—or postscript to all the different ways to protect against inflation in this book.

Now you have learned about all the different ways that you can protect your wealth, as well as build it. Everything you have read up to this point in the book has been about assets that you own directly.

And I believe that ownership and full responsibility is the most important thing when it comes to creating a free life and growing your wealth.

But I also recognize that there are investment personalities that are structured in such a way that they still don't want to take ownership, because it comes with the responsibility of your assets, and that means you have full control over them. If you are a type of personality that is easily overwhelmed with different possibilities, and also simply swamped in your day-to-day life, dealing with all the different problems, tasks, and operations, then all these different products we mention in the book on top of all that will most likely not help you sleep better. And I want you to sleep like a baby, just knowing that your wealth is growing even overnight while you sleep. So, to have this reality in your life, too, there is another Swiss solution that you can benefit from.

Think of Assetization as a tool. With it, you enter into the legislation of a financial product, which is different from the ownership of assets. Actually, it's not something I consider to be the best thing to do, but for the person who has problems with the feeling of being constantly overwhelmed, as I outlined above, it can be a suitable solution. If this is you, then Assetization might be a perfect fit for you. That's why I want to explain it at least in a nutshell teaching format: There is a process where a company brings in assets like art, real estate, or agriculture — maybe a plot of orange trees. This company brings these assets into a legal form and converts the whole thing into a financial product with a Swiss ISIN number.

What does this mean for you? You can still use your bank. You tell your banker that you want this or that ISIN number. You give them the amount you want to invest, and they manage to put all those assets into a financial product that the bank can handle in your portfolio.

Now you see why I don't think that's the best thing to do - because there's the bank! And there's the financial product—you don't really own it, you're just the bank's creditor. They owe it to you; and then, behind those links in the chain, there's the real asset that you see in your portfolio. It can be precious metals, it can be art, it can be value-added real estate; basically, it can be any of the assets that we have discussed before in this book.

That said, I hope you understand my point about ownership and financial products. It is okay if you still want to work with your bank while participating in the asset classes we discussed in this book.

When you want to test the waters of Swiss inflation protection without venturing too far into new territory initially, this is for you! You still work with your bank, you still have an officially licensed Swiss financial product with a Swiss ISIN number, and you can still participate in all the assets we have described.

SALES
CHAIN

Speed read: Life is constant change, and you need to cope with that.

If you want to become a smart Swiss Wealth Creation Investment strategist to navigate the ever-changing investment landscape and capitalize on emerging opportunities while managing risks effectively, being flexible and adaptable is crucial.

Things happen in life. Sometimes you need to sell some of your assets for an emergency, like a new car or a medical bill, and sometimes a great opportunity comes along, and you want to be a part of it. This is where having a diversified portfolio comes in handy. Diversification into different assets is one of the most important points. If you need money because of some unexpected situation, you may need to liquidate one of your assets. The more diversified you are, and the more different assets you have, the more choices you have at any given time to decide which of your assets you want to part with.

In a well-diversified portfolio, you can choose which of your assets you want to liquidate—some or all of them—

if your cash reserves are not sufficient. Maybe silver is high so you sell some silver, or bitcoin is high so you take some profits. Maybe you can sell a piece of your art collection or a barrel of balsamic vinegar. Or you can sell some company stock because the company is doing so well.

You always have options, and you never have the stress of having to sell at a loss! The sales chain is a powerful tool for optimizing your long-term profits and wealth accumulation.

When the price of gold is high, you sell gold. When the strategic metals are higher than the precious metals are at that time, then sell the strategic metals. Do you have diamonds, and are you getting a good price for them? Then maybe you sell the diamonds. Or, if you still have cryptocurrencies, you can sell some of your bitcoin holdings.

··

The more options you have, the better off you are with the whole sales chain.

··

It's a shame if you only have silver in your portfolio, and you have to sell it cheap if silver is at an all-time low.

When you still have a diamond on the side, maybe you can sell that.

Diamonds always belong in the portfolio if you have larger wealth to hedge against inflation.

When you have the sales chain in place, there's not a lot of money left in your bank account, which is fine. But what do you do when a good opportunity comes along; an opportunity that you want to be a part of? Well, you have to sell some of your assets. And it's important to have a system in place so that you know which of your funds you want to and can sell, and which you just want to keep.

The best case is always that you sell something at a profit when it's the right time to sell. You do not want to sell something when you would realize a loss, you want to sell something that absolutely makes economic sense to sell.

So, when that opportunity comes along, all you have to do is look at your portfolio and know which of your assets you want to sell some or all of in order to have some more funds to invest in a new opportunity.

Also, if you have a great network, and if you know people who are ready to invest, that's another way to avoid liquidating some of your assets - by bringing in new partners or existing partners to invest in the opportunity instead. So you can still keep your assets and build new assets, which is the highlight of your investment strategy. If you need to sell something, you just need to have a diversified portfolio so that you can pick one or some of your assets to liquidate, and not liquidate something that does not make economic sense.

What this means to you is that you have a diversified portfolio with multiple assets. You can evaluate your assets at this point in time and choose which asset makes sense to sell some or all of to get the funds you need, either for your emergency or for the next opportunity that is waiting for you. In this way, you always have different liquidation options, which makes your portfolio even stronger, because you can get rid of assets that have become less profitable, such as a stock where the company did not perform as well as the blueprint said it would. Or you can realize some gains if, for example, silver or a piece of art has increased in value. You then have the opportunity to exchange part of an asset for a new one that has greater potential or that will add even more diversification to your portfolio. The sales chain also gives you the opportunity to decide if you want to sell quickly because you need the money fast, or if you have some time left for the new investment and can prepare another asset for sale that will take a little more time to sell, such as real estate. Flexibility and market timing are the key words in the sales chain to optimize your portfolio while spreading the risks over more assets over time. You will always sleep well knowing that you have different assets to choose from when you need to liquidate to have funds for another opportunity.

I think we've just done a valuable job of putting some very worthwhile investment ideas on paper, but—and please correct me if I'm wrong, Reto—I think the best is yet to come. The bottom line, and the key to becoming a very successful investor, is to stay ahead of the curve. The only way to do that is through continuous learning, so I am convinced that every one of the investment opportunities you have already mentioned is very valuable, but the greatest value the reader will get is once he learns how to learn about financial growth.

Yes, Gisi, I agree one hundred percent. Above all, it's the right financial education that is needed to be ready to be your own bank!

PART III

THE THREE MOST IMPORTANT LESSONS

The three most crucial missions you need to complete:

1. Become educated!

2. Have a mentor!

3. Keep your expenses under control!

As you can see, there are many opportunities in the market that you can take advantage of, and believe me, we are only scratching the surface in this book!

....

There are so many things that are not widely known but that the really big players are always investing in, and now you have the opportunity to invest in them.

....

That's why it's so important for you to be financially literate. Financial literacy is a topic that unfortunately is not covered in schools. Students who leave school often don't know anything, not even the basics of investing, because it's just not taught. From my point of view, this is obvious, because who teaches in schools? They're employees, and they don't have the entrepreneurial mindset of someone who's really taking care of their own finances.

BECOME
EDUCATED

Speed read: Education is the key to unlocking personal freedom. (Only) by understanding how money works can you gain the power to make informed decisions, build wealth, and break free from financial constraints. It empowers you to take control of your future and create a life of independence and opportunity.

Reto, you just raised such an important issue. I'm holding back in this book because its purpose is, of course, the Swiss approach. But as I point out from time to time, my intention is not to better only a single country, but to help create a better earth. And to create a better earth for everyone, it is essential to have better education, so what I want to say is: you have just nailed it. You cannot educate others about things you do not personally know or live. How can a teacher teach children about abundance and wealth creation when he or she lives in constant financial scarcity? I'm not judging teachers, I'm judging a system that is nowhere near smart.

I think we all know that the subconscious of every human being is created between birth and about the age of 6. During that time, the young person just swallows up everything that comes into contact with them, and so their programming—all the subconscious programs that determine the entire rest of their lives—is realized! And when they are 6 years old and beyond, these "open vessels" close; the programming is fully done. After that, there are only lessons that come on top of these all-determining programs. So, in principle, it is totally crazy that the teachers who earn the most are those who are professors and teach in universities. There they have adults attending lectures who only get more knowledge, but the most important asset for a free and self-determined existence was completely done and closed years ago by others. This asset is your subconscious.

And this is not even *your* subconscious mind because of the simple fact that absolutely everything your subconscious mind tells you, you have received from others. Or have you had parents or teachers who consistently and systematically said to you, "Child, please make up your own mind. You have the right to doubt what I'm saying"? On the contrary, I bet you've also heard far too often, "Stop arguing and just do what I've told you!"

You received this programming before you were six years old. And you received it 100% from others. It is simply an inheritance. When you know that your own subconscious mind (again, not really your own because you got it from others and never had a chance to defend your own ideas when you were a little kid) is responsible for more than 95% of all your results in life, and that only

5% of everything you experience is created by your conscious mind (the one which is filled in at the university), you will agree that generally those who know how to really teach our youngest children should be the ones who earn the most!

My wife and I have two twins who are 9 years old as I write this. We have always been very conscious and fully aware of how their conscious minds are created, and so we are very carefully choosing who is permitted to feed the minds of our two children from their birth to this day. And this is something I want to transfer to this book, and ultimately to you, dear reader.

Who do you allow to teach you? Who do you listen to? Is it the banker who makes maybe 3 or 6 thousand a month who wants to make you believe that he knows how to advise you about how to become truly rich and financially satisfied? Or is it the teacher who gets much less money each month than they deserve for the great work they do? Are these the people who should be feeding your children's subconscious with financial wisdom? You better think again! Better education is a must to create a Better Earth, and instead of focusing on everything that is not working—wow, and there is a lot out there—let us focus on what is working:

You know, with all the noise and all the uncertainty out there, I have exactly two essential factors here that will undoubtedly work for us if we want to change the world.

> First things first: we cannot change the world. We must change *people* to get different results in the world we live in.

That means we must change the way we think. We must work on people's emotions and the things they do to create different things that we will all have.

So how do we do this? I believe the key is to reach out to the individual (not the masses) with some topics they are really interested in, and I guarantee I have two here that are most interesting to everyone on earth!

Yes, I know this is a big promise, but I will keep it; just stick with me:

The first thing that absolutely everyone has in common with everyone else is a gap! I am talking about the gap between the actual situation you have right now in your life and the desired situation where things are the way you want them to be. That can be better health, more wealth, love, happiness, and anything else that YOU want to enjoy in your life! And we don't have to go into the desired situation, we just have to see that really everybody has some desired situation that is totally different from the present reality.

So, it is not important what exactly the individual wishes are at this time. What I want us all to understand is that every single human being has this gap — the gap of not knowing how to get from the present situation to the desired life. If they knew how to do that, they would all be there and the gap wouldn't exist, but I'm sure you agree that this gap is just a fact.

The second is money. Money is with us every single moment of our lives, and even beyond: from our earliest years to our last day, and once on the other side, our loved ones have to pay for the funeral and take care of the estate. Therefore, money is definitely of great interest to everyone on earth—do you agree?

What if we could combine financial education with bridging the gap between your current situation and the lifestyle, health, longevity, abundance, bliss, love, and happiness you really want? Would you be interested in learning how to live your dream if there was someone who could teach you how to do it? Not because this person has read some fancy books, but because he has been living his own dreams for decades. Would you want to learn from this guy? Of course you would.

So, Reto, my point is that you have to be visible and show what you are doing so that others can see what you represent. The same goes for me and many others in our lives. Let's spread some hope and happiness and inspire people to want to know more about financial wisdom and a self-sufficient, good life in full autarky and self-responsibility.

You see, we live in a system that requires energy. There are some who profit from the fact that the masses are unaware of their own power and the forces at their command to change things.

My approach is to turn things around 180 degrees, and when we do that with our current system, the taking energy turns into a giving energy. The actual wealth pyramid, which represents the past, becomes a freedom pyramid, which represents exactly the opposite. Take a look:

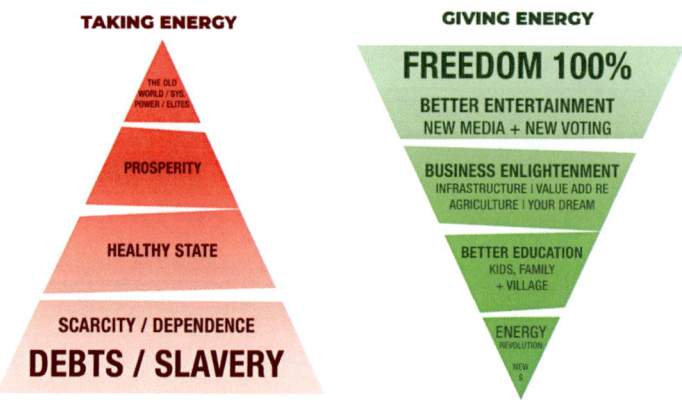

The second one, the Freedom Pyramid, is my business plan. I mean that.

So, when we start with new and sound money—which I also like to call money for freedom—and we succeed in investing in real green energy and better education, then the moment comes naturally when everyone who is involved also has the means to live according to their dreams!

And the next levels will plausibly emerge from natural dynamics; it will create business enlightenment, bring truth, better entertainment, better voting systems, and much better governance on Earth.

I will sum it up for you:

- **Better Economy**
- **Better Energy**
- **Better Education**
- **Business Enlightenment**
- **Better Entertainment**
- **Or just BE! Better Earth**

Let's connect and create it together.

Gisi: You just left me speechless! This is such a wonderful vision you have, and I believe there are many people like me who want to know more right now. What is the next step?

Oh, this is easy, Reto: Connection is the New Currency! Let's come together on *www.betterearth.be!* There will be ways to do this. But back to the main topic: financial education.

Exactly, yes. It is imperative that everyone educates themselves on this important topic.

You just have to see for yourself where you can get the best financial education!

For me, the most successful way to learn has always been to look at people who have already gone where I need to go. In other words, I have consistently and carefully focused on finding people who have been where I am now, but who are clearly where I want to be soon. They have to be people who understand my situation—a rich member of a royal family is hardly going to understand your situation if he doesn't know how you face a growth challenge for your own company... so it's important that I only take advice from people who a) have been where I am, and b) have a proven track record of getting the results I want.

I think it would be a good thing if the education system made improvements in this area and set out on new paths. But I am also aware that those who are still in charge may not want you to be financially literate, self-reliant, and free. You MUST take care of your own financial education. The same goes for your children and relatives, of course.

REGULATORS AND
REGULATIONS

Speed read: Our aim is not to criticize the existing environment, but to demonstrate how you can still engage in the lucrative game.

When we talk about education, there is one very specific topic that you cannot avoid. You need to learn the basics about regulations, and you should understand who the regulators are and why they do what they do. And even when you have this knowledge, it is best to work with some experts who can keep you out of trouble.

Reto, I am sure that you will fully agree with my following statement: Considering the overarching impact and long-term implications, the erosion of citizen rights and freedoms is by far the biggest problem for us all.

Yes, Gisi, and here we are with regulators and regulations:

We are in a time of storm. That is why we're writing *The Swiss Wealth Creation*. One of the real problems investors have to deal with are regulators and regulations. The financial situation of countries is critical. More and more money is being printed, and it looks like things are getting out of control. Yet the regulators want to protect the average Joe from investing in something he does not understand, so they create regulations to protect him. Well, this is the official version. It is certainly fact checker appropriate, and we are not saying anything sensitive. In fact, it is all about control. Remember the Energy-Taking Pyramid in the previous chapter! A good question leads to a better answer:

Have you ever asked yourself why the people in power are "protecting the little guy against risky investments" while their countries, whose regulators are their employees, are getting into deeper financial trouble every day?

Walk your talk! We do, but out there, teaching and living what is taught, in most cases, is very rare. Personally, when it comes to financial topics, I would only believe someone who has a positive P&L and is financially wise. When you see how countries dive into inflation and, at the same time, want to "protect" the citizen (the German word for citizen is "Bürger", comes from the verb "bürgen" = to guarantee; so the citizen is a guarantor for the state), it becomes more than grotesque.

You and I may not be able to change that, but we can respond by understanding what they want.

SEC
BAFIN
FINMA

These national institutions SEC (USA), BAFIN (Germany) and FINMA (Switzerland) are becoming more and more important for investors. Once they have an investment opportunity on their blacklist, it is very hard to get out of their focus.

I have learned that most of the companies that are blacklisted and accused by the German BAFIN for non-compliant behavior go bankrupt. Why would they do that? Because it is easier to declare bankruptcy than to deal with the BAFIN for months or years, with high costs and a negative result in most cases.

If you want to understand the regulator's motives, you need to know this: their focus is on financial products. This is where they want to protect retail investors. Once you become an accredited investor, you are out of focus. You must make sure that your investment is not a financial product, and if it is a financial product, you have to buy it from a partner that is compliant with the regulators and has all the necessary certifications. If you invest in a company where you think you are buying a real asset like a property, but the company collects the money and then buys a property, that is considered asset management and needs all the certifications. If the company does not have the necessary certifications, it can end up that the company must undo all the contracts as if they never existed. This can take a long time, and as I said before, most companies will go bankrupt in this case.

Also, if a product partner promises you a fixed rate of return, it is very likely that you are investing in a financial product. Again, make sure the product partner has all the necessary certifications to sell financial products.

To use one of my own mantras again, the regulators do not want the poor citizens to become rich with the vehicles that the rich citizens have!

Reto, this is exactly the point:

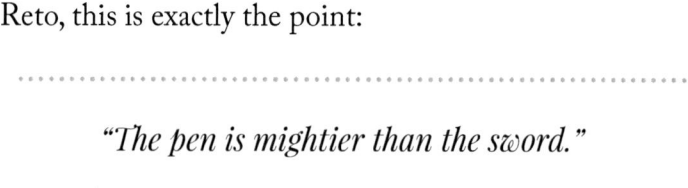

"The pen is mightier than the sword."

Regulators are indeed infringing upon the property and citizens' rights of hundreds of millions, if not billions, of people.

Again, this is a huge point for education; just imagine all these people learning and being aware of how they are being treated by those with a pen who sign these regulations. But I don't want to distract from the core issue here. Please go on…

Only if you know what you are doing, only then will you have the right to participate in the big business. This is one of the reasons why the rich get richer, and the poor get poorer!

My goal is not to blame the regulators, but to show you what you can do to play the rich game despite them.

Now that you know some of the cornerstones of the regulators, you can do a much better job of checking what kind of investment you are putting your money into and whether it is in compliance with the regulators.

There are laws to protect your data. And you have laws against money laundering. Let's put it in black and white: You want to sell your car for 20,000. You find a buyer who will pay you 20,000 in cash. Did you know that it is your responsibility to verify the source of the funds to the regulators if they ask? If you do not, it can be considered as supporting money laundering!

Just a side note - as we write this, the EU Parliament has banned cash and prohibited payments over 10,000 Euros! What does that mean, dear reader, besides the fact that you are no longer allowed to pay cash for anything worth more than 10K? Get in touch! The environment is changing fast—I don't know if I should compare it to quicksand or a minefield—but I am quite sure about one crucial fact: The changes are not in your favor. This book may not be up to date enough for you to find the latest information you need. Use the email Reto uses from time to time and really do yourself a favor:

Connect — see last chapter!

Back to money laundering and being guilty until proven innocent - Reto, please continue and sorry for the interruption.

Fine — so let us continue with the example that you sell your used car for 10,000 Euros. Now, if you check the source of the funds, you can be accused of not complying with privacy laws. Isn't that absolutely amazing? In fact, it is insane.

You see, either way, you lose! But what can you do about it? Either you sell your car to a car dealer, then it is their responsibility, or you work with a lawyer who knows how to protect you. I believe that nothing will happen if you do such a transaction once, but you need to be aware of what could happen and how you would react in that case.

Again, you need a good network of top specialists, such as lawyers and tax experts, that you can rely on when you need them. And you will need them. You will see why in the next few subchapters.

ABOUT BANKS AND REGULATIONS

Banks are like doctors: they protect themselves any way they can. You have to sign so many papers and paragraphs before you can do business with them. And they have the right to protect themselves even more if they must.

I think the banks do not want you to take money out of your bank account; they want you to leave it there so they can work with it. They put all these regulations in place either to protect you or to protect themselves.

Let me tell you a story: In 2017, I was involved in a lot of crypto projects. Those projects often had their bank accounts in tax and crypto-friendly countries like Belarus, Gibraltar (UK), and Malta. After sending and receiving funds to and from those countries, I was invited to a legal meeting at the bank. Sitting across from 3 bank lawyers, I had to explain to them why I was working with these companies in these countries. They wanted to know every detail about the business model and the partners. Finally, they told me that they would not accept any more of these transactions and threatened to close my bank account - an account I had with them with salary and other funds coming in every month for more than 30 years!

You just have to be aware of the regulations that banks have, and always have a Plan B. Right after the meeting,

I went to another bank to open another bank account so that I would have a choice whenever I wanted and needed to do another transaction.

Another bank that I use internationally has always been fine with my transactions. However, in their regulations, they mention that they do not support any transactions related to cannabis. For investments in legal medical and recreational cannabis, I have to use another bank that does not have those regulations.

ABOUT TAXES AND REGULATIONS

Taxes are another huge area of regulation. Most tax laws have a smaller portion of duties and a larger portion of exemptions. My goal is always to optimize the taxes I have to pay.

Tax laws have many exceptions and many paragraphs that can be interpreted differently. This is why you need a good tax advisor to help you optimize your taxes. This can be done in your own country, which usually makes the most sense. If you are dealing with larger sums, you can start looking for international opportunities. In general, these constructs are only recommended when the tax reduction is much greater than the initial and annual cost of such a construct. And you need to have a great specialist to help you comply with all the laws. Many people have moved to other countries only to find out that it cost them more in taxes because the setup was not done correctly.

A wise tax advisor can guide you to make appropriate decisions in relation to the value of your assets. Optimization can also mean paying regular taxes instead of building something expensive and saving some taxes! You must pay your taxes; just make sure they are optimized in relation to your assets.

ABOUT REGULATIONS AND MORE REGULATIONS

Finally, you need to know the rules. Or at least you need a strong team that knows the rules, such as accountants, tax advisors, and lawyers. When you do not follow the herd and leave your money in your bank account, then you need to take responsibility and find out where you have regulations and how to deal with them.

Most of the time, you will not be actively confronted with them, but the moment you are, you need to have your team ready to protect you and help you get out.

If those paragraphs scared you, then I have accomplished my goal. That is what these paragraphs are made for and why most people act the way they do: to avoid being confronted with them. Now that you know more about them, why they are made, and how to deal with them, you are ready to move forward, take control of yourself, and start investing in out-of-the-box opportunities!

GET A GREAT
MENTOR

Speed read: (Only) a mentor with expertise in financial matters can provide you with valuable insights and guidance based on their own experiences. They can share their knowledge about budgeting, investing, saving, and other important financial concepts.

A mentor can tailor his or her advice and guidance to your unique financial situation and goals. Your mentor will identify your unique areas for improvement, offer personalized strategies, and provide the best support for your financial decisions.

That's why I look for a mentor who is much further ahead than I am. I learn from them by figuring out what they did, how they got where they are, and what I can implement to become my own bank and continue to be my own bank.

You really have to educate yourself, and with that comes all the personal development and all the personal responsibility — two big and important topics for everyone who really wants to become outstanding. Because personal development is what you need to be able to position yourself very well in the market, to be able to buy and sell very well in the market, and to be able to value yourself in the best possible way.

You need personal development and personal responsibility to understand your counterpart better. And when you understand the people you are working with, you can continue to build your network in a much better way. Especially if you want to network with people who are more advanced than you are, you have to know that they want to feel that you are a personality they want to be around.

Yes, Reto, and from my own experience, the higher you go, the easier the personalities become to be with. The more successful they are, the more willing they are to share their wealth of experience and knowledge with you. And the reason for that is just natural. They just have a great attitude. And they don't have their extraordinary character traits because they are extraordinarily successful — they are extraordinarily successful because they have these extraordinary character traits.

And one of those qualities is that they are open to helping others. But do you think they would help anyone? I know they are very selective, but if you are the right person and you are in front of an extraordinary mentor, it will just change everything in your life!

It's rarely about your actual results, so don't make the mistake of thinking you have to be rich to get a successful, wealthy person as a mentor. This is complete nonsense, and they know it. It is all about whether you are open-minded, whether you show up with the right energy, and above all:

Are you teachable?

There is not a single successful person on earth-who has more experience than you in any area-who wants to be around the kind of person who already knows everything.

You are even less likely to get help from more advanced people if all you do is complain about your results. So be open-minded. Know that you simply don't know what you don't know, and rest assured that you simply must have the right attitude (not the financial means) to work with the best teachers.

"When the student is ready, the teacher will appear. When the student is truly ready... The teacher will disappear."
—Tao Te Ching

What this means for you is: The right teacher comes when you're ready. You are ready when you are teachable, when you are willing to learn new things, and not just to learn new skills, but to try and implement new things and make them your new unconscious behaviors.

Only then can anyone else help you create new results. And if it is not the case that you are already awesomely rich, then I would decide NOW to get rich—that is a new result. You must then become the person your best mentor wants to support and teach. In addition to your teachability score, which must be high, you must also have the right attitude. "With the right attitude, the facts don't matter!"

I will absolutely love to explain this statement to you in a one-on-one conversation, but we have a significant way to go before we can do that. Anyway, if you want to work with Reto and me, you should also be aware of the following:

Reto and I are expensive advisors. But that means that for the right person we can easily add a 10x, a 12x, or much more to your income level. But don't get this wrong: if you are looking for any guru to boost your health, wealth, and happiness,

… or if you want a get-rich-quick scam or any overnight problem solving…

… or if you want to get great results "cheaply" …

… or if you are one of those people who talk a lot about all the great things they want to do, but don't follow up with action…

… then this offer is definitely N O T for you!

We only work with open-minded individuals, so if this is you and you want more—not only for your business and your wealth creation, but also for yourself, your personal growth, and for the best effect for all your loved ones— and in contrast to the current times, for a better future and for the benefit of all, just remember to BE - like Better Earth…

… If you feel that there has to be more to life than a career leading to a "safe" retirement, and when you really want to dive into *The Swiss Wealth Creation* know-how and DO-HOWS…

… If you feel that you are one of those leaders who are moving our current reality into a wealth mindset-driven future that represents the fact that we are living in the highest abundance of all time…

… If you want to make purposeful gains and create a legacy of impact to generate great benefits for life…

… When you want to learn how to become a purposeful investor to systematically create more health, wealth, confidence, joy and longevity…

… Please connect with us via support@wgw-advisors. com and tell our team why YOU should be one of those individuals we would love to help with your wealth creation, sharing with you the most outstanding *Swiss Wealth Creation* deals on our table and—maybe, who knows—even establish a closer mentor-mentee relationship.

Anything is possible if you approach us with the right energy and drive!

Gisi, you just got me! I want that! Oh, my God, I am so happy that I am already one of your private mentoring clients :-) Yes, my dear reader—Gisi has been mentoring me for a couple of years now and I can only say: if you have the chance to work with Gisi on a one-on-one basis: do it!

I don't know if Gisi will be available when you read this, but what I do know is this. If you have the opportunity to work with Gisi, do it! He will absolutely change your life!

Because there is a tremendous need for much growth in the area of personality, and then it is quite natural to take responsibility for one's own financial resources.

Because only by taking personal responsibility will you be able to manage your life's financial satisfaction and make the necessary investments yourself, not leave it to a banker.

This is how you become your own bank, and then just remember the following at every moment: The world doesn't need banks. The world needs banking—and so do you!

Once you have a great mentor and do what he or she tells you to do, your wealth growth will be much faster. Be aware: Implementation is key! You will soon feel yourself taking on more and more responsibility, and as you do the right things over and over again—your mentor will hold you accountable for doing so—you will soon become financially independent.

With your financial independence, you are no longer dependent on a job! Just imagine: You can quit that job because your monthly income is generated from your investments in well-chosen cash flow projects.

Having a constant cash flow, without having to sell your time, gives you more freedom and much more self-confidence.

You will be free to do good things, and you don't have to ask anyone for permission.

Thanks, for the kind words Reto! That is one of the things I have learned: I am rich because all my life I have been doing what I want to do, how I want to do it, where I want to do it, and with the people I choose to do it with—and at this moment, I would like to say thank you, Reto. Thank you for this wonderful collaboration that we have established over the last few years. Thank you so much! You are a fantastic and inspiring role model of how to work together, achieve incredible results, create value for others and have a lot of fun doing it.

That's what I mean when I say, "Let joy work for you!" Here's a quick anecdote about this credo of mine: It was back in 2018 when I was reflecting on my last 10 years, and I was at the point of defining in writing who my perfect client is. At the time, I made a wish list in one of my journals of what my perfect client/mentoring client and/or partner looks like. They look like you, Reto. And I added that every text message I receive, every email that comes in, every time I hear from you, I will be more than happy to respond with your level of enthusiasm. And every time I get news from you, I will be happy about the developments in your life. This "you" is of course really addressed to you, my dear friend Reto, but believe it or not, you are in excellent company.

In 2018, when I got these ideas from one of my mentors, I literally thought, "Nice idea, but I don't think this is possible." We are now in 2024 and since 2022, my life is exactly as I described it in 2018. This "every message makes me even happier and more grateful" thing is 100% in place, and this is exactly the same in my personal life as it is in my business life. And those who are new in my life and don't fit into this reality, thank God, show their true colors very, very(!) quickly, so I can let them go in the next moment, and I do so happily, knowing that I've just avoided wasting a lot of time with people who don't appreciate me the way I honor and appreciate others and the way I want others to treat me.

So, once again, "Thank you, Reto, for being a perfect realization of these wishes I had 6 years ago."

And thank you to my mentor, Ed Rush, for putting these fruitful ideas into my head. Blessings to you both!

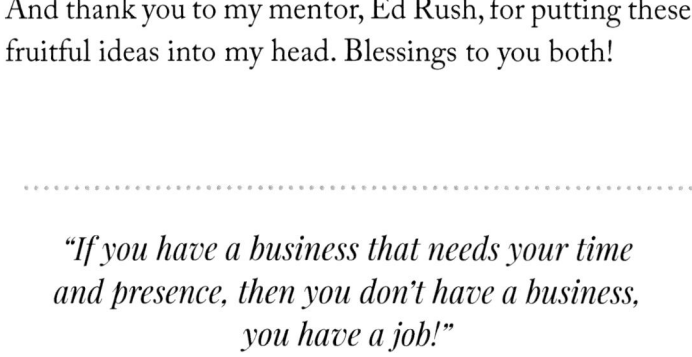

"If you have a business that needs your time and presence, then you don't have a business, you have a job!"

That's what Bob Proctor said to me in 2016, and I think that's exactly what you want to convey to the reader, Reto, when you say, "You can quit that job because your monthly income is generated from your investments in well-chosen cash flow projects." That's just a great feeling, isn't it?

Yes, Gisi, the confidence alone that comes with these accomplishments allows you to position yourself completely differently in every important area of life. You are here on a very positive mission, and you are being lifted up on a vortex of positive energy that is taking you higher and higher: Part of that vortex is that you have more money to invest each month. That's less expenses on the one hand and increasing returns on the other. Plus, the growing confidence will make you unstoppable!

Absolutely, Reto, and as you named this a "vortex of positive energy", I feel it is like an amplifier that just accelerates more and more wealth creation: This just happens naturally and on its own—I mean, there is no work required—the wealth creation goes on autopilot because of your growing self-esteem, self-confidence, unlimited confidence in a good life, and the absolute conviction that from the exact same source that all these amazing new results came from, more and more results will continue to come that will make you feel even better than you already do.

And believe me: you just feel greater and greater. This is the real magic of initiating this chain reaction, and the wonderful thing is that it is never too late to start.

KEEP YOUR
EXPENSES UNDER CONTROL!

Speed read: Keeping your expenses under control is critical, especially when you are experiencing significant income growth for the first time.

(Only) by maintaining disciplined spending habits can you avoid "lifestyle inflation" and build a solid financial foundation for life.

With all the exuberance of the last chapter, however, it is very, very important that you keep your spending under control, because if you allow yourself to become reckless, greedy, and overconfident, this whirlwind can quickly turn in a direction that is not good for anyone. There are two ways to ensure long-term financial stability, to allow for savings and investments, and to provide a buffer against unexpected circumstances.

You can reduce your expenses, which means you must get yourself under control, or you can increase your income proportionately.

Yes, Reto, and let me jump in with a time travel into the reader's future: Imagine that your income based on cash-flow projects and long-term returns accumulates and it becomes much higher than what you earn from your job. Now ask yourself: How long do you want to travel the world for beach testing? I bet you will enjoy it for a (hopefully long) while, but at some point, you will want to do something again. You will long for some great things to accomplish this because it is a part of your nature! Then it will be the case that you will work not for money but to do some amazing things. And you know what? Amazing things can bring amazing rewards. And since there is no need for it, it will most likely go through the roof, and your new work will skyrocket because you are now doing exactly what you want to do.

You are no longer blindfolded and brainwashed into earning money for a living. Now you are in the wonderful position of doing what is really most important to you, and you will see when you are there that this is exactly your sweet spot, where you can easily earn more than you can even imagine in your wildest dreams today.

This is another level of "work" — when you are in your essence, fulfilling your purpose.

You are here for a reason, and I wish that a large part of it is joy and beach testing.

Sun and sea views are great, but at the right time, you will feel your calling. Then follow!

Thank you, Gisi. Yes, I wanted to continue my thought with the idea that you can have a second job so you can earn more to invest more money and get passive income that you can then reinvest, or you can get more money in the job market if you are employed or self-employed.

So, there are two ways to invest more money—1) spend less, or 2) work for more money—but of course, your journey into the future is an image we like to stick to.

Let us conclude:
Learn to spend less than you earn.

This is the most plausible formula for becoming rich!

Another thing to remember is to always think in percentages. It's not important how much money you put away, *but what percentage* you can put away.

What percentage of the money that comes into your account each month can you allocate and invest in your growth? Your overall goal should be to increase that percentage. A classic example is if you get a raise of 200 francs or euros or dollars, next month you will have 200 francs/euros/dollars more in your total. This means that if you have been putting away 10 percent, that percentage will go down. It could be 9.8 percent or 9.5 percent after your raise. That's why I always suggest that you calculate in percentages what you can really put aside to invest.

Reto, since we are with this 10 percent example right now, and I believe that consistently setting aside 10 percent of my income and investing it in my financial growth is a wonderful idea, let me ask you a question that I believe the reader will also be wondering about: What would be your best practice? How do you allocate that 10 percent across the different investment categories that we talked about? How do you allocate your investments in a reserve, in asset protection, accumulation, and cash flow projects?

An optimal distribution is 10 percent in reserves and then 30 percent in asset protection, 30 percent in asset accumulation and therefore projects, and 30 percent in real estate. I think that is the ideal allocation. Of the individual assets, I recommend not having more than 15 percent in any one asset, and also to keep the risk there as low as possible. Something can always go wrong.

That way, if I don't have more than 15 percent in any one asset, I'm already very, very well positioned. Ray Dalio says if you get 15 solid income streams and look for uncorrelated assets, you don't limit your upside while avoiding large drawdowns. That's why I say, as a guideline, with 15 percent as a cap on an asset, depending on what situation I'm in, how many assets do I have? What is my strategy? But as a rule of thumb, I would say 10, 30, 30, 30 percent.

Another very important point is: what percentage of your expenses can you already cover with passive income? The goal is clearly to keep increasing that percentage so that it is over 100%. This way, you are financially independent because you have more income from your passive income than you have expenses. And that should be the first major milestone for you - to become financially independent. In other words, it's about increasing your passive income as a percentage so that it reaches 100% of your total expenses.

What we've seen with all these projects is that most of them are independent of each other. That is, they are uncorrelated, and the larger your portfolio of uncorrelated assets, the better positioned you are for the future. There are going to be changes in our economy, in our lives, in the whole financial world, in the political world. What matters is how you are positioned when those changes hit you. And the more assets you have that are not correlated with each other, the more secure your financial position will be when we experience major changes.

INVESTMENT
CLUBS

Speed read: You ignite the turbo when you are together with like-minded people. One very special option is to join an investor club.

This means that we, the like-minded people, join forces - and that has advantages. We can exchange ideas. We speak the same language. We have the same interests. We have the same investments. And we can invest money together in larger projects that bring even more and better returns. That gives you greater access to big projects that you might not be able to get into as an individual, either because you don't have the financial means or because if you did get in, the cluster risk would be far too great because it would take up too large a proportion of your total assets. Hence, the investors' club. There we can minimize all the risk.

With the Investors' Club, we learn together, and we go into areas that we can't or aren't allowed to go into on our own, and that's how we've created the next turbo to really build up our portfolio even faster, in addition to the fact that we can also access many other new investments through the Investors' Club, because then you're no longer alone at the table. We are perhaps 5, 10, 15, or even 20 people, and they all bring good deals to the table. We then discuss them with each other, continue to build up our financial knowledge, filter out the best deals, and move forward together. And yes, drive the whole thing forward with a team and take the next steps. This will enable us to achieve this financial independence and passive income for our economy as quickly as possible.

PART IV
WHAT CAN BE YOUR NEXT STEP?

CONNECTION IS
THE NEW CURRENCY

Part IV is the final part. Actually, calling this part the "Final Part" is the opposite of what it really is. In the best of all scenarios, it is now the beginning of something truly groundbreaking and new for you!

....

> *The Swiss Wealth Creation* deal flow is in a constant state of change. It is of utmost importance to be connected to take full advantage of it.

....

The connection we are talking about is much more than just expanding your business network. It's personal. Motivational. Powerful. Practical. Our in-person and online training sessions advance your investment strategy by creating a strong alignment with the overall theme of growing your wealth, and you get a full-scale boost to realize a breakthrough in your financial satisfaction and freedom.

NOW
YOU HAVE
TO CHOOSE!

There are only three options (which make things very easy for you). Here they are:

1. *Do nothing with what you have learned.*

2. *Take what you've learned and experience how to make it on your own.*

3. *Enjoy more and more of these teachings, take advantage of our experience, and let us guide you every step of the way to becoming an excellent Swiss Wealth Creation investor.*

You've gotten this far by reading this entire book. You're probably not here for the first option, which is to do nothing with all you've learned in this book. So, my guess is that you are way above average, and you are not here just to be entertained. You're still reading because you want to keep learning, you're here because you care about all our futures, and you're here because you want to accomplish more with the right people in the right places.

You want to be successful on a much higher level!

You're not here reading the last few paragraphs of this book just to waste your time out of curiosity. So, I know option number one is really not an option for you.

For those who put the book down 100 pages early, that might have been an option, but they're probably not above average either, right? But you are because you're still here.

So, I think you're probably going to choose the second or third choice. You're probably going to take what you've learned from this book and try to do it on your own. We support that. If what we've just shared with you inspires you to the point where you can do it on your own, then Reto and I are glad that we got to spend this time here with you, that we got to share some good investment ideas with you, and that you are taking away the resources and skills that absolutely can help you make it. Because that's what we want for you!

But if you are one of those who feel that you want to share the path with Reto and me, because you want experienced companions who have walked this path many times and can guide you, then you don't want to walk it alone. You want great helpers! You want support from personalities who really walk their talk, and you may feel that you are not ready to do everything yourself. You want to be able to work in a protected environment with proven systems and processes that work for you and are appropriate for your wealth, without having to spend a lot of time on trial and error, right? And you don't want to do it wrong.

Especially when it comes to transformative processes—and growing to new shores of abundance is a huge and powerful transformation—it is important that those who guide you have been through many, many, many, many (there could be more "manys" here but I believe you get the message!) transformative, profound processes many, many, many,…, many times, and I mean many(!) times, and have helped other people do this successfully countless times.

Your e-motion (energy in motion) is the most important key factor on your path to great wealth, and it is 100% dependent on how you think and feel.

This means that your belief in yourself, your belief in your accomplishments, your attitude, and your mindset are much more important than your skills and how you act. The intangible, your inner world, determines 95-99% of all your results—including wealth and value creation—and the conscious part, your skills and knowing how to use what you have learned, determines only 1-5% of your results. Of course, the combination and the right deal flow is extremely important to create the whole picture.

When I tell you that, together, Reto and I have successfully guided hundreds, if not thousands, of people through their processes, you will probably want to take the third option.

So, if you are one of those who know that great success is only possible with commitment, if you not only appreciate valuable advice but also like to implement new things, and if you want our proven *Swiss Wealth Creation System* to help you become a wealthy investor and live a life worth enjoying for many more years with better health, more impact, more joy, less stress, and much more confidence, then this is EXACTLY RIGHT for you:

· ·

Connect with our team:

support@wgw-advisors.com

Tell our team why YOU should be the next person we help.

· ·

Have a wonderful time and let *The Swiss Wealth Creation* work for the best of your results. It was our absolute honor and pleasure to share our thoughts and expertise with you. Thank you for reading:

Reto Winkler & Gisbert Reuter

ABOUT THE
AUTHORS

RETO WINKLER

Is a renowned consultant specializing in alternative investments, known for his deep expertise beyond traditional bank and insurance products. As a savvy global investor, Reto identifies and capitalizes on solid, high-yield, long-term investment opportunities that are truly out of the box.

With over 20 years of experience in financial education, Reto has served as a teacher, coach, mentor, and co-investor in numerous non-correlating investment ventures. His passion lies in real assets and discovering little-known investment opportunities. By providing access to these opportunities for both institutional and non-institutional investors, Reto empowers individuals to create wealth tailored to their unique needs and possibilities.

Reto's approach centers on asset protection and growth within a diversified portfolio, ensuring sustainable financial development. His expertise has helped hundreds of clients embrace innovative financial strategies and achieve remarkable results.

Reto Winkler's services present a range of diverse, proven global opportunities designed to achieve a 15% return with ease. With potential returns spanning from 12% to 48%, many investments exceed expectations, demonstrating Reto's commitment to high performance and excellence in wealth creation.

What clients are saying:

"Reto is one of the most knowledgeable people I know in this topic & 100% trustworthy. HIGHLY RECOMMENDED!"

Jason Gilbert, CEO Mentor & Hyper Growth Advisor. High-Impact Business, Political, and Philanthropic Game Changer. Jason retired to spend more time with family, and now mentors other CEOs and ultra-high achievers on three continents. He specializes in power branding, hyper-growth strategies, and leadership.

"Reto Winkler is an absolutely prudent and trustworthy partner when it comes to gaining a new and profitable perspective on finances.

A goose that lays golden eggs? Until I met Reto Winkler, I would never have thought that possible. He accompanies his clients with a great deal of expertise into what may still be an unfamiliar world!"

Ursula Arn, Expert for change and reorientation, mentoring, training and coaching.

"Reto Winkler is an outstanding financial specialist. In his lectures and seminars, he teaches the basics of wealth accumulation in a way that is simple and easy to understand for the layperson. As a cash flow trainer and cryptocurrency specialist, he helps people to build wealth sensibly and achieve financial freedom. I can recommend Reto Winkler to all people who are seriously interested in taking responsibility for their own lives and financial freedom. He is someone who really lives what he teaches!"

Gerhard Schobel, Speaker, Trainer, Empowerment-Expert.

GISBERT REUTER

Gisbert Reuter is a 4-time international #1 Best-Selling Author, Award-Winning Creative Director, Mentor, and Partner-Advisor to 6-, 7-, 8-, and even 10-figure business owners. Known affectionately by his seminar participants as the "Millionaire of the Hearts," Gisbert's clients often express deep gratitude for the transformative impact he has on their lives.

Living a life of adventure and inspiration, Gisbert, along with his wife Gina and their twin children, splits his time between the Canary Islands, South America, and the picturesque German island of Rügen in the Baltic Sea, where he runs his Private Mentoring Center.

At just 19, Gisbert made the bold decision to live abroad, and by 24, he had relocated to the Canary Islands. Long before the term "digital nomad" was coined, Gisbert was pioneering this lifestyle. In 1998, he founded his first media production and marketing company in the Canary Islands. By 2000, he was leveraging "geo-arbitrage"— earning an income in London while enjoying the lifestyle and lower costs of the Canary Islands. This strategy evolved as he worked with clients from Switzerland, Gibraltar, Germany, and beyond, eventually earning in Europe while living in South America, achieving up to a

"20-X" increase in income by residing in affordable, idyllic locations.

Throughout his illustrious career, Gisbert has focused on helping people realize their true potential and leave a lasting legacy. His mantra, "Let Joy Work For You," embodies his approach to both life and business.

Over 30 years in the industry, Gisbert has assisted more than 10,000 individuals, both online and offline, in achieving their desired results with ease and joy. His clients and cooperation partners include global top players such as the former Vice-President of Warner Brothers TV Prod, the President of JVC-Victor, Japan, and renowned film industry story consultant Michael Hauge, as well as consulting legends like Bob Proctor.

Gisbert Reuter's journey and expertise make him a remarkable figure in the world of creative direction, mentorship, and business consultancy.

What clients are saying:

"An example to the world" — Marc, Banker, Barcelona, Spain

"Gisbert is the mentor I have always wanted: a person who is close to his students, transparent and clear as water, warm and authentic." — Rubi Espinosa Business Owner in the Fashion Industry.

"Talk to Gisi. if he can't help you, nobody can!" — Ed Rush. 5-Time #1 Best Selling Author and Amazon's #1 Business Author, San Diego, USA. Ed's clients range from small startups to multi-million dollar – multi-national organizations and include CEOs, founders, political leaders, sports teams, national universities, and Hollywood stars.

"Working together with you Gisi, the whole experience, has been terrific for me." — Michael Hauge

Top#1 Best Seller Author and one of Hollywood's top consultants and story experts. Hollywood, California, USA. Michael has worked with countless screenwriters, novelists and filmmakers. He has consulted on projects starring (among many others) Will Smith, Julia Roberts, Tom Cruise and consulted some of the world's most successful online marketing experts.

"The amount of work and incredible people in this book is remarkable. The experiences, wisdom, thoughts, inspiration, and motivation is priceless." (About the book World Unlocked, written by Gisbert Reuter & Friends) —Brian J. Esposito

CEO of Esposito Enterprises. With a $16+ billion track record, he is among the Top-10 CEOs 2020-24. Global Business Leaders Mag: "Top #3 in the Top-10 Admired Companies Which Everyone Should Know."

"From the 1st moment, you are completely picked up and feel 100% understood. Gisi has an extraordinary gift for you. In his heart, there is eternal summer; he makes you laugh and gives you courage, even when you feel like crying. An inexhaustible, honest source of inspiration."

— Nicole Pellinen

Real Estate & Livestyle Luminary, Hamburg (Germany) and Marbella (Spain).

"My life will never be the same!"

— Zeida Evangeline Coro

Lawyer, Guatemala City.

IMPRINT

THE SWISS WEALTH CREATION

A Comprehensive Guide For a New Era of Investment

Reto Winkler and Gisbert Reuter

First edition: September 2024

ISBN: 978-3-949109-34-8 (Paperback)
ISBN: 978-3-949109-36-2 (Hardcover)

All rights reserved.

Copyright © 2024 Reto Winkler and Gisbert Reuter

LEAP PUBLISHING

Leap Advancement Germany GmbH • Colonnaden 5 • D-20354 Hamburg. Registered at Hamburg Court HRB 158497

Made in the USA
Las Vegas, NV
12 January 2025

09469b42-1813-489e-a4be-73888205ab13R01